THE SOUL SEARCHER
SCENES FROM MY LIFE

written by Judy Fraser
Spiritual Psychotherapist

Copyright © 2011 Judy Fraser

Published by Landraagon
Design & Illustration Pavllou Landraagon
www.landraagon.com

ISBN-13: 978-91-979875-0-9
ISBN-10: 9197987506

THIS BOOK IS DEDICATED
TO THE GARDENERS
OF THE EARTH

AND TO
MY FOUR CHILDREN,
THE BEST TEACHERS I COULD EVER
HOPE TO LEARN FROM

Acknowledgements

With special thanks to:
The Management Upstairs for supplying all copy and illustrations and so strongly encouraging the author to make the material available.

Richard White from Word Edit: Professional
Literary Services, the editor of *Second Aid*.

Pavllou Landraagon, Publishing Agent and Cover Designer.

Alex Amengual Newletter, Distributor and Website Maintainer.

Gordon Volke and Richard Hall the editors of *Second Aid*'s
companion book, *The Soul Searcher*.

THE FLICKER AND THE FLAME

'TWIXT THE SWEETNESS OF LIGHT
AND TRUTH OF SHADOW
STANDS THE FLICKER AND THE FLAME
COME FORTH INTO
THE FOREST'S DARK CANOPY
THAT COVERS OVER BLAME
WITH DARK BLACK EARTH BELOW
AND TREE TOPS HIGH HEADY BREW
AND FALL SURRENDER INTO IT
TO THE ANCIENT TIME ANEW

FEET COUNT STEPS
TOWARDS THE DARKNESS
HEARTS BEAT TOWARDS THE LIGHT
NOW BE IN FRONT OF THE MISTY GATEWAY
OF THE DAYTIME AND THE NIGHT
NOW COME TO STAND BETWIXT
THE FLICKER AND THE FLAME
MAGIC WHISPERS AT THIS DOORWAY
TO NEVER BE THE SAME

Chapter 1- Shapes in the Fire

My earliest memories are ones of utter isolation and loneliness so absolute they were tangible. What was I doing in this strange world? Where were the people I was supposed to contact and connect to? Being born didn't feel like being alive – it felt more like dying to all that I had known before. Picking up the atmosphere surrounding my birth, I detected the unhappiness and worry of my mother and those advising her. A tiny baby is not supposed to remember anything of this time, but my memory remains as clear as a bell. Certainly, I had no idea how I was supposed to respond. Nor was I thrilled about being so vulnerable, but what could I do? Better just try and get on with it.

Taken away by a kind, nice-smelling lady, I was left in the care of an orphanage after my birth with a view to adoption being arranged. I thought this would be in the stewardship of the nice-smelling lady, but no! I was placed in the care of the people who ran the home and the lady disappeared. This was towards the end of World War II, a time when there were far too many orphaned children and not enough resources or people to care for them. So, every weekend, many disparate people showed up – married couples, single men, single women. Virtually anyone willing to take on the care of a child was allowed to have one with the minimum of fuss. Whenever this cattle market took place, attendance for us was compulsory! Week in and week out, some children were chosen and others rejected. For months and months (even years) I was one of the ones rejected. This never disappointed me as the world I knew appeared safe. The unknown did not. I was happy to stay at the orphanage where I felt I belonged.

Then, one Saturday, my turn came along with another girl called Jane. She was just two years older than me. Much later on, I found out she was in care because she'd been abused by her parents. Jane was emotionally damaged by this and found it very hard to relate to anybody – especially me. Anyway, having had my cheeks rubbed with a pumice stone and my hair treated to a few flicks of a comb, I was considered to look healthy enough to take my place in the market parade. On this particular Saturday morning, a wide range of people paraded through the room, peering at the children like you would peer at strange and unrecognisable animals at a zoo. Comments were made in front of us children as if we were deaf and blind and a bit thick. Did these people not understand we were vulnerable little people with powerful emotions?

Then it happened! We were chosen! The kind, nice-smelling woman came back and I found myself being transported to the home of a lady called Elsa and her highly nervous grown-up daughter, Betty – whether I liked it or not! Betty was there to greet us, taciturn and unfriendly – or so it seemed to me. Elsa appeared to rule the roost, yet she was warm and friendly. Betty, on the other hand, was more like someone from Victorian England. Resentful of her mother's popularity and her easy manner, the daughter appeared bitter and reliant on the services of others.

It seemed that money and comfort were not issues at my new home. It was a nice five-bedroom house standing in its own garden. It had a live-in, full-time help, plus a gardener. It appeared very comfortable at a physical level, but it was cold emotionally. Jane and I shared a nursery. I knew immediately that she was hostile towards everyone, but as time went on we appeared to be able to agree to differ and we rubbed along. Very early on, I was acutely aware that she had to cross my half of the room to reach her own half. When she came into my space, it appeared to change and the atmosphere became tarnished somehow. That was the extent of her emotional negativity.

There was a coal fire kept permanently alight as my health was not good. The most comfort for me came from the shapes that appeared in the soot at the back of the chimney. These little fire-salamanders became my friends and they brought me hope. So did the breeze in the trees outside and the cloud pictures I saw in the sky. I escaped into their care as often as I was able. That was quite a lot as I was a sickly child. Bronchitis was a constant problem and I had double pneumonia three times within a few years.

Even when allowed out of the nursery, Jane and I had to keep clean so as to be presented in the drawing room each evening at six p.m. We were looked at, spoken at and shown to others who might or might not be present for an endless hour, after which we were sent back to our room. We were looked after by Eileen, a wonderfully warm, understanding and motherly lady who was not yet 30 herself. Without her, I would have been sunk. She fed us and allowed me into her kitchen to watch her work while sitting at the kitchen table. On other occasions, suitably trussed up, I was allowed to venture forth into the garden. Only just walking and still a bit unsteady on my feet, my life took a turn for the better. I met Mr Blake, the gardener, who was not supposed to talk to me but did. He became my hero. I followed him around and he talked to me while he worked. Learning about soil content, what flowers went with what, how to plant vegetables so they supported each other's growth – I was in my element and felt content for the first time since arrival on earth.

Once, taking a tumble down some stone steps, I cut my forehead and narrowly missed my left eye. Sporting stitches and a heavy bandage, I was banned from exploration and had to stay within sight of the lounge window whenever I was in the garden for a long six weeks. The little freedom I had tasted and the nurture from the land were withdrawn from me almost as soon as they were experienced. Yet my deep love of nature began to develop; a peace and nurture that has supported me for all of my life. Combining nature with my friends in the fire, I felt it was possible to know a contentment that I was humbled by and deeply grateful for. Even at that young age, I decided to try to unite the outer visibility of nature with my inner feelings to provide some kind of instruction that would help to navigate my passage.

The older lady, Elsa, started to call herself Granny and soon became more approachable. She saw my developing love of books and nurtured it by talking to me. I recognised her sense of fun and plucked up the courage to present her with a bag of coke wrapped up to look like sweets on April Fools Day. She was amused and kindly, but Betty did not think it was funny at all. Told it was dirty, naughty and cheeky, I was banished to the nursery for days. Meals were brought to me as I was no longer allowed into the warm kitchen or to talk to Eileen. This experience and my general exposure to people did little to encourage me to interact better, but the next thing was I was being told I had to go to school! Jane was excited while I was filled with dread.

The only experience I'd had of lots of people being together was seeing a refugee camp on some downs nearby. Everyone seemed to scuttle by and not respond to comments or requests for information about this place. Often they pretended these people were not even there. Food rationing was still a fact of life and all children had to have disgusting thick orange juice, malt extract and cod liver oil. You had to be taken to a large building full of children along with a guardian who had to prove your identity. Then you got a dosage on the spot and more to be taken away and administered from your place of residence. If this was what school was to be like, I did not want to be a part of it! Yet, in spite of my extreme misgivings, I found myself dressed up in a uniform and delivered. Standing in the playground and looking around, I was horrified. All my senses jarred. Girls talking, some shouting, some running around! It was a blur of energies all mixing and intermixing. Talk about total overload! I just could not make any sense of this scenario. Maybe it would be better when we got inside.

Before long, we were herded into a room, assigned a desk and a chair and told to sit down and take notice. Beneath the high windows and with little view, I studied the interior and the other children. The teacher sat at a bigger desk on a raised platform behind which was a huge blackboard. The children sat in rows one behind another, new kids towards the front of the classroom. Each child appeared to have a greyish appearance that extended anywhere from one to ten centimetres or so beyond their skin. What was that all about? The teacher also seemed to have fuzzy edges. When there was movement, it all seemed to appear like a fog. Very strange! How ever was I going to survive and endure? Perhaps it would be best to try to switch off and to withdraw inside of myself. I would concentrate on what little sky I was able to see and wait until able to get out. Now feeling a bit dizzy and sick, I was being picked out by the teacher and expected to respond. Asking to be excused, I made the doorway before being sick and fainting. Coming round, I found myself the focus of the class's attention – not in a good way, either. I decided I was going to hate school and the only way to manage it was to 'be good' and do as I was told and just wait until I was able to get away. Speaking with Jane in the afternoon after school, I felt even more confused. She loved the experience and was full of being able to interact with other children and the excitement of learning. I wasn't!

Settling down and later finding out I could excel in things that interested me, I was totally unable to concentrate or focus on anything which did not. And a lot of what was being taught seemed to me to be not the things I wanted to learn. Games lessons were an especial nightmare. There seemed to be times when people took the opportunity to criticise and condemn various bodily attributes being displayed when changing and then to beat one another up on the field. We were encouraged to compete and challenge. The members of staff were as bad as the children. Lunchtime and breaks proved to be a watered-down version of games lessons. Feeling more lonely by the day, this was clearly something to be endured. So it was time to find out how others were managing. Obviously, I wasn't doing very well myself. Everyone I spoke to did not seem to understand my hatred of school and obviously thought me to be deranged. Was I? What was wrong with me? I was beginning to look pale and wan and was putting on weight despite not eating much. What was going on? One bad dose of bronchitis followed another. Then, at least, I was allowed to stay at the house and in bed. The local doctor was called Dr Spratt. He was nice and kind. He lived nearby and had twin girls a little older than I was. He seemed to understand me and to identify with my condition. Was he going to act as a lifeline to me? He went off to speak to Betty and her mother and for a few days they seemed to make an effort. Soon, however, it appeared that the disruption caused by my illness was considered to be a nuisance. Although Elsa had been the instigator of my removal to the house, her daughter Betty was the official guardian in the court's eyes. I don't know, but I think Elsa thought it might motivate Betty and give some sort of function and purpose. Eileen brought food which I did not want to eat and drinks I left untouched. Dr Spratt visited and brought medicines which made little difference either. For hours on my own, I talked to my invisible friends and asked them for advice and for help. A peace was found in these times, but not much help. Pneumonia followed and removal to hospital. Even though very difficult to get hold of in those days, a teddy bear was given to me which I loved, cuddled and talked to frequently. During this time, I had the oddest of memories. I was never sure if they were real or imagined. I saw myself being carried down a long, white, sterile hospital corridor to go to see a man swathed in bandages. We stood there staring at this unconscious form for what seemed like ages. Then I was carried back down the corridor and found myself in bed with my teddy. I was certain this man was my real father and that he was dying or dead already but who could I speak to and ask? No one. So I didn't!

Once recovered, I returned to the house and – joy of joys – was let out into the garden for a while in the hope that some colour would return. Then I would be able to go back to school – oh great! But still the trees, flowers, grass and earth brought stillness and Mr Blake was pleased to see me. I loved him so much! What you saw was what you got. His outgoing kindness reflected from within him and there were no double agendas or difficult to understand innuendoes. As my verbal skills began to improve, I started to ask him about himself and his life. He told me he lived in a small two-up, two-down house and he was poor.

"Is there a Mrs Blake?" I asked.

"Yes, there is," he replied and he spoke about her with such love, I started to cry. He let me sob. He did not touch me. Instead, he just stood there in silence until I was able to stop, surrounding me with love.

"Do you have children?" I continued.

"Yes, two," he answered, again speaking with such pride and love!

"Can I come and live with you?" I asked.

"No," he said, gently. "We all have an individual pathway and yours is here."

"Why?" I sobbed.

"Just because…" he murmured. He stood leaning on his garden fork, regarding me with deep sympathy as I stared into his face. Having been told many times not to talk to Mr Blake but to leave him to get on with his work, I wandered off to watch the poplar trees swaying in the breeze. They seemed to be whispering to each other and to me. Later, I caught Mr Blake speaking with Eileen as he delivered vegetables to the kitchen door. I know they were talking about me. Maybe with Mr Blake in the garden and Eileen in the house, I would grow up and be well in spite of myself. Just knowing they were there made me feel I could cope with the school system. At least now I was willing to try.

A pattern began to emerge – a time at school, a dose of bronchitis, recovery time in the garden and back to school. Surprisingly, I kept up with my school work and developed a love of reading. I was encouraged to listen to the radio, but found I preferred listening to what others thought was silence. Silence to me was filled with sounds from the wind, the trees, birds and nature. Also within that silence came things to watch and to see, such as the flames within the fire, soot at the back of the chimney, and pictures in the clouds. They all carried messages that were familiar to me somehow. When radios blared or people talked loudly, they disappeared.

Jane and I talked when we were together, but we couldn't communicate. She seemed to be obsessed by the weather and little else and I found that boring. She clearly thought I was bonkers when I asked if she could see shapes within the fire. We rubbed along together, but we had nothing in common except for living in the same house. One day, Betty decided we should learn to tell the time and we knelt in front of this chiming clock. I remember this experience clearly. Jane and I sat either side of her while she explained the hour and the minute hand, the quarter hour chiming and making a lovely sound. Both of us picked this skill up very quickly and it was over. The only other time I remember close contact with Betty as a child was her coming into the bathroom one night and telling us about being adopted. She went on about having to tell us as she was not married and she did not want us to be embarrassed at school – too late for that! She talked about the war, the number of kids needing homes, how lucky we were, how her brother, a vicar, approved of her action and so it went on. Not much was said about where we came from, who our parents were and nothing about how we might be feeling, but lots about her. That may be a little unfair, but it was certainly how both Jane and I experienced it when we spoke of it later.

I asked Jane how she felt about her parents. "Aren't you curious about them and where you came from?" I enquired. "No," she replied, simply.

I was, however, extremely curious to know about my origins, but soon learned that it was useless to ask. After a few tries, the subject was dropped. Harangued for being selfish, ungrateful and dissatisfied, I stopped asking and let the matter rest. It was frustrating not to have the verbal skills or the physical strength to persist with something I felt to be my right to know. I felt powerless and imprisoned in the web of other people. In spite of the nice house, there was little warmth or love displayed within it, or so it seemed to me.

Out of the blue, Elsa and Betty arranged a holiday for themselves to Salzburg and Vienna. Jane and I were to spend five days in a children's home and then Eileen, who was away on holiday herself, would return and care for us for the following two weeks. The children's home was nice enough. In fact, for me, it made me question whether we would have been better off being brought up in a place like this rather than being adopted. If you behaved yourself, you were left alone by the authorities in the home and just allowed to be who you were. This created a camaraderie with the other children who were in the same circumstances as you. They looked out for each other all the time. It was rather nice and a lot less lonely. No need to feel sorry for yourself here as everyone was in the same boat. No need to explain circumstances for the same reason. Maybe I was ungrateful, but I enjoyed it enormously none the less. Under a week and we were back at the house. But was it the same one? Eileen was there and pleased to see us – genuinely. Also, she had a boyfriend whom we did not know about and he came to call often. There followed the best two weeks of my life! The house was transformed with fun and laughter. The atmosphere was permissive and tolerant. What a difference! Mr Blake came into the kitchen for coffee rather than staying outside. The banter between him and Eileen's boyfriend made all of us laugh and we were all happy and relaxed. We were touched and hugged for no reason, something we had never experienced before. It was a wonderfully relaxed and happy interlude.

All too soon this idyllic time was over. Elsa and Betty returned. The last thing I want to do is to be unfair to them as they had their own issues to confront. Elsa had been the wife of a famous composer of his day and had mixed in a society where Green Rooms were as familiar to her as a cup of tea is to others. Her house had been filled with the arts and artists of the day. After the death of her husband and the long years of war, her life was a stark contrast to what it had been before. This must have been so difficult for her. She became a home warden and did the best she could for her son, Guy. He was the vicar, a married man with three children. Betty became her mother's companion after a wartime love affair. Now she was an unworldly woman landed with two evacuee children and a mother who was getting older and more frail by the day. She had a love-hate relationship with her mother, but was not brave enough to openly rebel or stage a revolution apparently. She allowed herself just to be swept along by events.

Was it natural for one as young as I was to think about these things? I was often experiencing my own feelings as well as the feelings of others — or so it seemed. It appeared I was 'reading' these feelings well enough. Often I got a strong and unexpected response when I dared to voice or question something. I soon learned not to do this and to keep things to myself.

The normal round resumed — school, bronchitis, garden, a little additional freedom being found in learning to ride a bike in amongst the maze of the rose garden. Somewhat painful on occasions, but well worth the effort! The garden was laid out well. It had a large vegetable garden with an underground air raid shelter within it. It was never used in war-time, as there was not the time to get to it, the dining table and the cupboard under the stairs being the favoured areas of shelter. The garden also had a herbaceous border, lawn going up to trees and a sandpit made from the large pond that had been there before my arrival. Then there was more lawn, a rose garden, a further lawn and then the gate and the shingled parking area for visitors. Provided I did not go out of the gate, I now had the run of the garden, bike or no bike.

One day, a lady who was familiar to me came to visit. She was the nice-smelling lady from the official round between birth and adoption named Mrs Rose Lampson. She was paying a call as Granny was not too well. I was in the garden recovering from yet another bout of bronchitis. As Mrs Lampson was leaving, she stopped to speak with me by the crab apple tree at the gate. She seemed a little furtive and anxious that anyone watching from the house should not catch on. She said that she had some information that she felt I needed to know. She had been instrumental in putting my adoption through and she wanted me to know my father was a Canadian serviceman over here training for the Dieppe raid. My mother came from the Isle of Wight. As far as she knew, they had both died which was why I found myself in the position of needing care. She then put her hand on my arm in a secretive manner. "Please do not tell anyone I have told you," she whispered.

"Okay," I agreed. "But why?"

"Because it would not be approved of," she replied, seriously. She put her hand on the wheel of the bike to show anyone watching that we might have been talking about tyre pressures. Then she smiled and left.

Later, I *was* questioned as to the content of the conversation. Following the lead I had been given, I said we were discussing the bike. Feeling dead inside, I retreated into myself behind the willow tree where a hedge sheltered me from being watched. So I was an orphan and not to know my history. Did it matter? Perhaps not! I was lonely anyway and there was no one to discuss this information with, so what could I do? Better to appear as normal and to avoid any difficult discussions.

Granny Elsa got worse and was confined to her room. Betty stayed with her and on the rare occasions she emerged it was to tell us to be quiet, the nursery being next to Granny's bedroom. Betty was very irritable and poor Eileen suffered. The atmosphere in the house was extremely tense, to put it mildly, with everyone having to creep around. Guy arrived which was a rare occurrence, Betty having a difficult relationship with him. She seemed to treat him more like a partner than a brother and this was obviously discomforting to him, his wife and his family. Guy showed up in our room and began talking about leaves falling off the trees in the autumn. This was his way of getting around to Granny having passed on. I felt a bit sad but Jane did not appear to be so. She did point out that this event would bring significant changes, but neither of us realised at the time just how much or how many. Now aged eleven and nine respectively, we were not allowed to attend the funeral. We just watched the cortege leave the house and return a few hours later. We were confined to the nursery where a very over-busy and overwhelmed Eileen brought us a drink and a sandwich. We tried to quiz her, but she was way too rushed to stop and speak to us.

Then Guy came in. This was a good chance, I thought, to discuss the matter of life after death. Possibly not the most tactful timing considering his mother had just died, but I went ahead none the less. I told him I believed that life was continuous, whether dead or alive. We just did not understand how to relate to it. He looked at me as if I had lost my mind. He told me I didn't know what I was talking about and stated that he had nothing to say to me other than I should not think I knew about things spiritual. This was a bit rich, I thought, seeing as we were dragged to church every week and had to go to Sunday School as well. I wondered if he thought their teaching was a waste of time? I wisely kept my mouth shut as he left. Stating my opinion strongly to Jane, she was just not interested and told me to shut up. I watched out of the window as people left, trying to figure out who each one was. Jane did not bother with that either.

What was to come now? Well, more than I had bargained for! We were told that the house and the garden were to go. Mr Blake was to be released and so was Eileen. And the excuse was me! I was not happy with this at all. Dr Spratt had once said that I would fare better in Devon or in Switzerland where the climate would be good for my general health. So the great sacrifice was being made on my behalf and we were to move.

The idea of not having Eileen in my life, nor my beloved Mr Blake, was intolerable. Eileen told me it was her chance to marry her boyfriend and to have children whom she wanted more than anything as a result of her association with us. That helped a little. I was glad she had a chance of happiness. She had certainly earned that. The idea of being alone with Betty and Jane in a strange place filled me with apprehension and horror. But there was nothing I could do to stop it and there followed a time of watching the house and the garden being dismantled. Lots of things were sold or given away. Other stuff was packed up and, all too soon, the day came for us to leave in an old-fashioned car with running boards. Scarily, Betty was driving. This was something she rarely did and even then she only drove a few miles. Jane and I were not impressed by her driving skills and this seemed to be a journey that would last forever. We were going to a house we had never seen in a village we had never heard of a few miles from

Sidmouth in Devon. Then, the following week, we were due to start in a new school we hadn't seen either! What would become of us?

Chapter 2 - Men And All That Jazz

With a few stops along the way and very frayed nerves, we made it to our new home. Having lived on the outskirts of a large town, we now found ourselves in a tiny village. Driving down a lane, we came to a pretty little house that was sideways on to the road. It was a one-up, one-down cottage with a large extension added onto the side containing a spacious lounge with two bedrooms and a bathroom beyond it. The garden was pretty and had a stream running through the middle of it. It looked like something from the cover of House and Garden magazine – but would it be a home?

Mr and Mrs Collins greeted us. Mrs Collins had been employed for two days a week to clean the house; Mr Collins the same to care for the garden. Mrs Collins had made a meal to greet us. She was a friendly soul who did her best to make us feel welcome. However, Betty was dismissive and we were not prepared to give up Eileen's place in our hearts as yet. Poor woman! The meal was nice and most welcome, despite our ingratitude. Betty was to have the bedroom above the kitchen in the old part of the house. Jane and I would have a bedroom each in the new annex. We were pleased with this arrangement as it was the first time we'd ever had our own bedrooms.

Enough furniture was in place for our first night. New beds had been delivered and the kitchen table and chairs had been purchased from the previous owners. The main furniture was being brought from the old house and was due to arrive next day. Mr and Mrs Collins helped with the unpacking and the distribution of goods. Jane and I also wanted to take a much more active role. So, with four of us working and Betty supervising, there was order by end of the day. We were given some time off to look around the village and explore the garden. Upon our return, we discovered we were expected to cycle to school the next day.

We had been enrolled at a private school situated in an old and beautiful manor house. It took us 30 minutes to cycle there on that first morning. It was uphill and neither Jane nor I were used to cycling anywhere other than round the garden or the road outside the house. When we arrived, we were hot and dishevelled. We dumped our bikes where we were told and reported to the Head's office. We found ourselves standing in an oak-panelled hall with an impressive staircase and portraits of people looking very austere staring down at us from the walls. The Head swept down the stairs, gave us a pep talk, then dispatched us to different classrooms in the care of two pupils who had been summoned to escort us. We could see this was going to be a very different experience!

It turned out to be a very eccentric place! Run by two sisters, the Le Paiges, they did not seem to be teachers, yet they ruled with an iron hand. Were they part of the family of the old Manor House who had insisted on staying? Or were they really teachers who had come as part of the school when it was evacuated from Weston-super-Mare? I never knew. Discipline was strict and there was no nonsense during lessons or games. Having missed so much school, I was behind – but not for long. I was expected to work hard and also play games. It became clear very quickly that I didn't like competitive sport and I hated hockey in particular which was regarded as a great sin. The Games teacher did not like me, but tolerated my playing on the wing where I did little to help or to harm. One day, a ball hit me hard on the hand, breaking two bones. So, happily, I was excused from playing for a while and placed in the care of the Maths teacher who was called Miss Woodward. She'd had a bad accident in which she'd lost one leg. Unsurprisingly, her nickname was 'Pegleg'. She tapped her way into class with a silver-topped walking stick. She always wore beige or brown and seemed quite colourless, having beige skin and hair to match. She also had big spectacles and a lined face that rarely smiled, but on the rare occasions when she did, her face completely lit up.

No games meant extra Maths teaching. This was not a bad thing for I was well behind in this subject. Miss Woodward was very formidable, but also a brilliant teacher. Over the coming weeks, she managed to get me up to standard and then even a little ahead. She also prised out of me a bit about the situation at the house which was deteriorating fast. At this time, neither Jane nor I could work out what was wrong. We just knew that Betty never seemed to be available and we could never find a reason. She had all day at her disposal and Mr and Mrs Collins were constantly in and out. Yet nothing ever got done. When we got back from school, Betty was always taking a rest. We were capable enough of making ourselves a snack, doing our homework and watching TV, but we began to notice our lack of care. We wondered why. I had no more chest infections for over a year, but some allergy and sinus problems had started instead. They were controllable and treated by the village doctor who was called Dr St Cin. At his surgery, he told me he'd met Betty and if we ever needed him to give him a shout. I thought this was a bit odd, but I dismissed it as the local GP extending a friendly welcome to village newcomers. The church was almost next door to our house and attendance was statutory, so we met and socialised with others who were attending Sunday services. Betty's status gained a boost when Guy visited with his family. He was now a rural Dean and an important visitor attending our service.

Guy said he'd come to check up on Betty who had appeared a little odd on the phone and also to see if we'd settled in. He told us he'd left his phone number with Mrs Collins in case we needed to get in touch with him urgently. Again, we thought how nice, but not much more than that. I had made friends with the horses up the lane and spent a lot of my time walking to see them. Jane was into pop music and spent a lot of time in her room, listening to records and the radio.

Coming home from school one day, we found Betty on the floor, having been sick all over the lounge carpet. Cajoling her and telling her off (a complete reversal of our usual roles) we managed to get her to bed. Then Jane and I fought about who would do the cleaning up. I lost and tackled the revolting job while she got us something to eat. This was not to become an isolated incident, either. Eventually, Betty's behaviour became the talk of the village. Drinking at home...drinking to get to church...drinking before going shopping...buying booze at the local shop and then going on to town for more and so on. Betty was out of control. She was a disaster and an accident waiting to happen.

One day, seeing the fabric of the home falling apart at all levels, Mrs Collins told me she was going to phone Guy the next day. She never got the chance. That night, Betty fell heavily and banged her head on the kitchen table. Not being able to rouse her, I called Dr St Cin who came immediately and called an ambulance which took Betty to the local hospital. Being thirteen and eleven respectively, Dr St Cin considered Jane and I were too young to be left alone and took us to his house where we spent the next week. His wife was so kindly and his children were most welcoming towards us. We became a part of a normal family and, although it took some getting used to for everyone concerned, it proved a wonderful respite.

None of us knew it at the time, but this interlude set the pattern for the year to come. The St Cins moved into a bigger house at about the same time that Jane and I became constant visitors. I was a lot better at dealing with illness and accidents than Jane was, not being nearly so squeamish. So it became the established routine that I dealt with Betty while Jane did everything else that needed to be done. We began to dread what we would find on our return from school each day. Mr and Mrs Collins were as supportive as they could be, but there were limits to what they could do. After all, they had their own family to deal with.

Having been in and out of the local hospital on umpteen occasions, the day came when Betty started telling everyone about the pink elephants that were climbing up the walls. That was enough! Dr St Cin called Guy and they agreed that Betty should be sent to dry out in The York Clinic, a specialist unit at Guy's hospital in London. She was diagnosed with depression and underwent a large number of ECT treatments, keeping her in hospital for just under three months. On being told she was back and we were to return to the cottage with her, Jane and I both cried and were filled with dread. Life had been so domestic and normal with the St Cin family, we both wanted it to continue in the same vein.

At this point, it was decided in the interests of all parties that the cottage would be best sold and a move to the town just three miles down the road should be instigated. Betty would have to get out and about a bit more and there would be more people to keep an eye on her. She had rekindled an interest in painting while in hospital and was down to attend the local art class. Jane and I were also growing up fast and would have access to the sea, sport, more of a social life and be able to do the shopping when necessary without having to he driven. This move necessitated another new school, of course, but Miss Paige and Miss Woodward did a lot of important liaison work on our behalf. Sometimes, people can be so nice and so kind. The cottage sold quickly and for a good price, allowing a two-floor, three-bedroom maisonette to be purchased. Facing the local cricket pitch beyond which was the sea meant that the view was lovely. It was a Regency terraced block, nearly all broken up into apartments except for the small family-run hotel next door.

Downstairs from us was a warm, twinkly eyed lady called Mrs Murphy. She seemed very 'normal' and friendly and talked a lot about raising her own two children, often telling us what they were doing now and where they were. She also talked a lot about her hobbies, what she did and where she went. She was the widow of the man who started Murphy's television. We all shared the hall, but nothing else. On the first floor there was a kitchen, a small lounge and Betty's bedroom. The lounge and the bedroom both had a balcony across the front, facing the cricket pitch and the sea. Upstairs, on a half-landing, was the bathroom, then up another half-flight of stairs to our two smaller bedrooms.

I was to attend a boarding school located at the back of the town as a day girl. Jane had to go to Sixth Form College. Within a few weeks of starting at my school, I got such a bad allergy and sinus infection that I was taken to hospital in Exeter and ended up having an operation. It was too far for Betty to visit, so a hospital visitor was assigned to me, but there was no real need because, in spite of the pain, I was having a ball! Being the youngest by far, the other patients made a fuss of me and teased me about my two post-op black eyes. I was having great fun and loving every minute of it. One night, in pyjamas and dressing gowns, we went across the road to a pub that we could see from the ward window. We thought we were being really daring, but the publican told us it was an everyday occurrence and all his customers were well used to it!

My health visitor, who was called Josephine, had a son called Tim and ran a jazz club outside of the city. She invited me to be a regular at the club and I was determined that I would be. It was a dreadful shock arriving back home. Jane had been having a rough time on her own with Betty and now expected me to do more than my share to make up for being away. Jane had begun a relationship with a long streak of a guy called Dennis and this had caused mayhem because, being an electrician, Betty did not think him to be suitable. Guy had been summoned and poor Jane had been read the riot act. To me, it seemed to work like an animating force within her. As a result of this conflict, she became better company to be with. She was told that, if she did not stop seeing Dennis, she would be sent to Domestic Science College some distance away in Dorset.

To escape the house, I started to play tennis. This was very handy because the tennis club shared its premises with the cricket club just beyond our window. I also started Scottish country dancing as a result of an invitation from a member of a local demonstration team. I loved both. Tennis and dancing allowed me to get out more and mix with 'normal' people. Life in the house was not so good and life at my new school was bland – again with the exception of one teacher. Miss Reiner stimulated me enormously, not only regarding the English she taught me but also for her impeccable dress sense and make-up skills. She was warm and easy to talk to. She was as willing to talk about fashion as she was about classical literature. She had eclectic taste and was flexible. As a result of that, a great deal was learned without anyone realising that was so.

Having been absent a lot and a new day girl, the other children in class tolerated me but did not make friends with me. I was not allowed to do any cross-country running or play hockey, but I excelled at netball and tennis, captaining the school teams. So the other girls came to accept me, unfortunately just before I was due to leave. I also gained infamy for fainting in assembly. It seemed I did not like being in crowded spaces where people appeared to press in on me.

A favourite activity of mine away from school was going for long, solitary walks on the cliff tops and then sitting down and staring out to sea. It brought an inner strength and a comfort and had a familiarity to it. It appeared to me much more spiritual than the rituals of the church regime. All that people appeared to do there was gossip about each other's appearance and this offended me in some way that I could not fully understand. When we were there, Jane and I used to eye up the choirboys and discuss their merits afterwards as it seemed to be a younger version of what everyone else was doing.

Arriving back at the house one day after school, all hell seemed to have broken loose! Jane was in tears and Betty and Guy were closeted together like old mother hens. It seemed that Jane was still in a relationship with her electrician and it did not meet with their approval. Jane was disgusted by their class-consciousness, as was I. She was told there was to be no discussion. Dennis was history and she was to be sent away to a Domestic Science College. Jane said that was fine, thinking Dennis would find a way to rescue her. She appeared to conform and be compliant, so peace was restored. But it was all an act. I knew that and forced her to admit it to me. The adults seemed to think they had spoken – therefore, it was so!

One of the Scottish dancers was a captain at a local army camp and had decided to teach his son Adrian to drive on the base. He asked me if I would like to join them. I jumped at the chance. Now sixteen, I thought it was a great idea. Betty was so preoccupied that she agreed and so every spare minute I had was spent in this manner. I applied to take my test three days after my seventeenth birthday and passed with flying colours, as did Adrian. Driving myself down to the local coffee bar directly afterwards in the Mini we had both used to take the test, I promptly reversed the car into another one while trying to park! There was minimal damage, but it was a good lesson for me.

Driving gave me a sense of much needed freedom. Meanwhile, Jane was in deep trouble at home and was being sent to the Domestic Science College in Dorset. She was bitter about this, but I felt jealous that she was escaping and getting away from it all. I thought it would be good for her...and then I realised it meant I would be alone with Betty! I was sure she was drinking again, having found a bottle of sherry secreted in the kitchen where she painted and she seemed to smell of it more often than not. She said it was the sleeping drug prescribed by Dr St Cin, but I was not so sure.

The day came when Jane was to leave and I drove her to Dorset using Betty's Ford Popular that she no longer used herself. Jane looked very woebegone, like a character from a Dickens novel, and I really felt for her as I left her at the College and drove away, promising to come back and see her soon. Not long afterwards, I left school myself with the headmistress's comment ringing in my ears: "Not much of a brain, but what there is appears to be very well balanced."

Now I started a year's secretarial course in Exeter some miles away. Travelling by bus, the journey took an hour each way and I spent six hours a day at college. Betty told me to use her car as she wanted me back at the house. And, yes, she was drinking again, but trying desperately to hide it. When at home, she was so clingy and demanding that it made me feel claustrophobic. So, at every opportunity, I got out of the house. She was not the only one who was depressed. I was going that way as well in spite of lots of physical activity.

Then I met an Indian medical student called Junior. It was like manna from Heaven! We walked and talked for hours. We discussed life, culture, religion and for the very first time I felt understood. Betty was shocked and disgusted. This inter-racial relationship was a far greater crime than an electrician, it seemed. We were getting closer and closer until Junior made the mistake of telling his parents as well. They also took a very dim view of our relationship and withdrew his funding because they already had a partner lined up for him. So, for his seventh and final year, he was taken back to Mumbai, or Bombay as it was then called. I was shattered! So was he. And Betty was furious too. It was okay for her to disapprove of us, but for them to do the same – that was beyond the pale! Deeply disgusted but not really understanding why, I walked the cliffs and had a quiet time with the ocean. I needed to get back to cloud gazing and communicating with the world of nature.

At this time, Betty still went to church on a Sunday and expected me to go with her. She did not want to go to the local church where she was known, so I drove her to a lovely church at the back of the town. Directly I walked in, I sensed the wonderful atmosphere of the place. It was so beautiful, so pure and somehow so familiar to me. This felt so much where I wanted to be that I actually passed out. This was not to be a one-off occurrence, either. Later, when Guy took a locum sick- leave cover for the vicar, we went every week and it was always too much for me and I fainted. Embarrassed, Guy told me to drink tea and eat biscuits and not to fast prior to service. That was no good. The church wardens got used to carrying me out, laying me on the gravestones and waiting for me to return to everyday consciousness. This never happened in other churches. What was going on? It appeared the church somehow answered the homesickness that was a constant companion, but how? I often wondered about that.

Each night, Betty took a very strong prescribed sleeping drug which, combined with alcohol, knocked her out by 9 p.m. So I took to attending the jazz club that had been introduced to me by Josephine, my hospital visitor. There I met Mike. He was a little older than me and, to my surprise, he was wowed by me. He had two artificial legs, yet was an agricultural surveyor and walked miles each day and then danced at night. I was so impressed by his courage, we fell into an innocent and rewarding relationship and spent every spare minute in each other's company. One day, he went into Roehampton hospital near London to have an operational adjustment on his leg stumps. He rang me to say he was on his way back. Then he walked to the end of the ward to collect something, collapsed and died instantly.

When he did not turn up, I could not understand it. After three days, I was frantic. Then I received a call from his wife! Boy, did she do a number on me! It was understandable, but so very hurtful. Apparently, they had two children together. She had found my phone number and some notes that had passed between us in his clothes at the hospital. She told me she had suspected he was having an affair. He had never told me he was married and I suspected nothing. He appeared available and free as a bird. His wife was very accusing and, as she continued to rant at me, something died inside at the seeming injustice of it all. Betty's comment was: "Well, you weren't married to him. You'll get over it!" That did nothing to console me. What did that have to do with anything?

Josephine and Tim were very supportive. I began working for them part-time at their guest house where the jazz club was held and that helped a lot. Tim was very funny. Once, he lay in wait for his mother and me at the bottom of the stairs with a daffodil sticking out of his bare buttocks. Unfortunately, it wasn't us that came down the stairs but another guest. That made it even funnier! Then there was the time he tried on a nightdress that had been left on a bed and the guest caught him. All of this helped me through my grief and despair at losing Mike, yet there was worse to come.

I became anxious about using Betty's car every evening in case she noticed the mileage going up and my involvement with the jazz club was discovered. So, one evening, Tim collected me in his car but said he could not take me home. A regular we nicknamed 'Juke-Box Johnnie' offered to give me a lift instead. He was called this as he traded juke-box machines around the area. Knowing he was married and my town was on his way home, none of us thought his offer was anything but a kindness. Yet he parked in a remote area on top of a cliff and began to kiss me. I was horrified and tried to get out of the car. I was more than prepared to walk the remaining three miles or so to get away from him. But he was way too quick for me. He chased me, caught me and then raped me. Still being a virgin and with no men around the house, I knew nothing of sexual matters. I was deeply shocked, hurt and bleeding. Afterwards, Johnnie obviously experienced guilt and became super-conciliatory. He drove me straight home and dropped me at the end of the terrace. Numbed and sickened, I stumbled into the house.

Never had I felt the lack of parents more! Why, oh why, did they have to die? Since earliest childhood, I had felt the energies around me as my father and the earth as my mother. Right now, this connection seemed to have been severed and I wanted the attention of the earthly variety, solid loving people. I felt abandoned and so very alone, locked in my pain. Knowing Betty would be drugged and out of it by now, she would be no help. So I put all the soothing salts I could find into a hot bath and lay in it and cried. Eventually, I dragged myself out and put all the clothes I had been wearing into a bin bag to be deposed of the following day. Then I went to bed to cry the night away. Next morning, Betty noticed nothing wrong, even though I was creeping around the house and being very quiet. A lecture on being out too much and not available for her was all I got from her. I realised there was no point in expecting sympathy from anyone, so I decided to lay low for some days to come. Josephine eventually telephoned to find out where I had got to. Sensing my distress, she came to see me. She told Betty we were going out for a walk which we did. Gently and sensitively, she got out of me what had happened. Without her support and care at that time, I might well have gone under.

Soon things began to really hot up at the house. Betty started falling about when drunk and Mrs Murphy from downstairs began to be worried. The noise of the stumbling and the shouts when Betty fell were disturbing her. The ambulance men began to know me by name, they had to call so regularly. Mrs Murphy remained as sweet and kind as ever, but she was elderly and vulnerable. When Betty nearly set the house on fire one day, she decided something had got to be done if we were all to survive. So she called Guy. I was relieved to see him, thinking the problem would now be solved. Imagine my surprise when he soothed Mrs Murphy, gave Betty a bit of a talking to, told me to keep up the good work – and left!

I had now finished at secretarial college, having passed typing and book keeping but failed dismally at shorthand. What was I to do with my life? My lack of direction felt highlighted when Jane phoned to say she was coming over. She had finished with Dennis, her electrician, and had met another man called Eric on a placement she had taken up after college. She was coming to say goodbye. Eric was an Englishman who'd lived and worked in Australia for many years. He was over here on a one-year specialist course for the Australian Coastguard Service and was due to go back soon. Jane was going back with him and they intended to get married in a few months' time. On her departure, she said she would keep in touch with me and help me whenever she could, but she never intended to have anything to do with Betty, Guy or his family again. Good as her word, she did keep contact with me by the occasional letter right up to Betty's death many years later.

Dr St Cin now called twice a week and was as supportive and kind as always. This was something Guy had instigated when he saw Betty. It placated Mrs Murphy and always gave encouragement to me. One day, the doctor left Betty in the lounge and took me into the kitchen. "What are you going to do with your life now, my dear?" he asked, kindly. "You can't stay or you will be here for years and years and become an old maid."

"I can't leave," I replied, bursting into tears. "I'm trapped. There's no way I can leave Betty in this state."

"You must leave," he insisted. "I will take responsibility for Betty. If you don't get out now, you never will – and you must! Betty can go to a place where she'll be supervised. You can't do it any more. It needs more than one person to manage this situation now. And I will call on her once a week."

A frantic few weeks followed. Dr St Cin told Betty he had arranged for her to stay at a lovely home. Much to everyone's surprise, she seemed pleased at the prospect. She perked up hugely when the maisonette was put on the market. We sorted out the furniture she would take with her and what would be auctioned. It took weeks to sort through all the stuff, many people coming and going. The car was sold to a local garage. They commented on the high mileage. I looked the other way when Betty said she could not understand it. The car had not been used for years apart from shopping trips!

Everything was ready and Betty went happily to her new home. I was seventeen, alone and independent! With the help of a contact of Dr St Cin's, I got a job working in Warwickshire. An optician he knew wanted a secretary/receptionist. With two suitcases and a heart full of hope, I left on the train having said a fond goodbye to dear, kind Mrs Murphy and Dr St Cin who drove me to the station. I cried when I left him. He and his family had done so much for me over the years and I owed my freedom to him. Although I wanted it desperately, I was scared.

I lasted eight weeks in this first job. Accommodation had been arranged in a house next to a railway line. A nice couple called Bill and Marjorie Evans allowed one person to rent their attic room to help with the cost of caring for their severely disabled daughter, Megan. Unfortunately, the house literally shook to its foundations every time a train went by. As this was hourly, and I wasn't used to it, I didn't get much sleep. As a result, I was late for work every day and not at my best when interacting with the optician or the customers. Even I could see I was a liability, so I wasn't surprised or saddened when I was asked to leave.

I had heard that Roy Wise, Prospective Parliamentary Candidate for the Conservative Party, wanted extra secretarial help for his agent during the forthcoming election. After going for an interview, I was lucky enough to be appointed straight away. This was just what I needed in order to pay my rent to Bill and Marjorie and for the evening meal they gave me. I did not want to let the family down. They were being so kind to me, even though Megan was extremely unwell. Eventually, I got used to the trains and, being given later starting and finishing times, I flourished. Loving the buzz and the excitement of this busy office, I settled in quickly. They seemed to like me and the work I did on their behalf, so I started being given more social duties as well as my other work.

A full-time youth worker called Tom was brought in from Leamington Spa to help with these more social activities in the hope of attracting the young to vote. He and I hit it off straight away. We worked well together and had a common interest in being more effective in our communication with the youngest section of the voting public, all of whom were older than me and only a few years younger than Tom. We had good fun and seemed to be thrown together more and more. For me, it was a crash course in learning how to be young and being able to let go of some of the care-worn aspects of life that I had experienced.

Election Day arrived. Having had so little sleep over the weeks prior to the election, I went into the chemist and asked the pharmacist to give me something to keep me going until after the count. He did this and I sailed through the day. Roy Wise got in and the celebration continued through into the early hours. Tom walked me home, gave me a kiss and told me to sleep well. Did I ever? 30 hours later, he was called round to find out if something had happened to me. It had! I had completely crashed out after the upper given to me by the chemist had worn off. My landlady woke me and none of us could believe that anyone could sleep for that long. And I still felt tired! Never again would I take an upper because the natural downer that followed was just too severe!

Tom returned to Leamington Spa, but I stayed in Rugby – although we saw each other as much as we were able. A few months later, Tom called to say he had got a job as a full-time agent in London and he wanted me to go with him as his wife. First he was to spend six months in Birmingham and he wanted me to join him there when my job finished in another three weeks' time. He left and got digs in a lovely, friendly house and he found a room for me in Handsworth, just walking distance away. So when I found myself there a few weeks later, I felt very pleased. My only regret was leaving the lovely Evans family in Rugby. This was especially difficult because, a few days prior to my departure, Megan died and I felt I was betraying them by leaving. They were always so unselfish and supportive of me right up to the end. Maybe they were relieved to be able to grieve in peace without me. I just felt so sorry and so impotent as I moved on with my life.

The embittered dragon of a new landlady was a very different kettle of fish. She was the only single lady and her house divided the black community and the Irish community which made up the street. Tensions were tangible in the house and outside. She said she knew I was engaged and that Tom could visit me during the day, but must leave the house by 9 p.m. each night as she would not tolerate any inappropriate behaviour. Wondering whether it ever occurred to her that inappropriate behaviour could be had during daylight hours amused both of us. However, none took place as I was too scared of physical contact (although I never told him why). He bought me an emerald engagement ring. Then said he had to go away up north as a part of his work commitment. I was not best pleased at this and threw the ring back in his direction. It plopped into a pan of spaghetti I was cooking. We laughed a lot as we fished about in and eventually found the ring, none the worse for its immersion! It did teach me never again to throw a fit of temper and lash out.

Working in a local factory, I caught the bus to work each day. One day, when the bus was full and I was standing, the conductor turned sharply and I caught the ticket machine right in the stomach. Not feeling well on arrival at work, I vomited suddenly and then fainted. The company nurse called an ambulance and I was taken to hospital. After quizzing me and finding I had no relatives anywhere nearby, the police were sent to apply to a judge to gain permission to operate for an emergency appendicitis. Still a couple of months away from eighteen, I was unable to sign for myself. This time, I wanted Tom more than wanting parents, especially after a doctor decided to examine me more than once in an inappropriate manner. Despite feeling really ill, I told the ward sister. Imagine my shock when she told me there had been three complaints against this same houseman in recent months, all from young girls. What happened to him, I do not know. All I know is that I signed a statement the sister gave me at the same time that the police arrived with signed permission for the operation to take place. So I was taken straight to theatre.

No keyhole surgery leaving a neat little scar for me! It looked like the porter could have done a better job. Septic scar, stomach pains and infection kept me in the hospital for ten days. The ward staff had found out about Tom, traced where he was working and told him what had happened. He arrived at the end of my first week with a huge bunch of flowers and a broad smile. In another ten days, I was just about able to stand up straight and not look as if I had an overwhelming desire to study my toenails as I walked! Going into the city on my first big outing, we went into an up-market cafe for a cup of coffee. I visited the Ladies and washed my hands, taking my ring off as I did. Then I left the wash room, leaving the ring behind.

Realising what I'd done, I rushed back — and to my astonishment it was still there! In years to come, I wondered if it was a missed signal, but at the time I was so bull headed that it did not occur to me.

Telling Betty the news that I was getting married put me in a terrible conflict. I didn't really want to tell her at all and I certainly didn't want to see her, but I knew I couldn't get away with either. So I phoned her and told her of our plans. Because Jane had gone away for her wedding, I felt I should ask in spite of myself if she would like to attend the planned Registry Office wedding. Of course, she said yes. Oh dear! She would come up with a carer and they would stay in one of Birmingham's top hotels. She would sign any papers required. It sounded like relief that she was getting shot of me at last. That felt to me like a grave miscarriage of justice given the circumstances of the last few years. Tom and I were to leave for London the same day as the ceremony and would stay with Tom's mother in Morden near Kingston-upon-Thames. He said his mother was too old and fragile to attend the ceremony and would celebrate with us on our arrival at her home. The night before the big day, Betty duly arrived and was well into drinking Brandy Sours by the time we joined her. I had never had one before and after just two I felt quite legless! Tom fared better, but we soon decided to leave, saying we would meet with her and the carer again the following morning at the Registry Office. Just before we left, I got a long lecture that I should be marrying in church with Guy officiating. On saying I could not promise to stay with one person for the rest of my life when I did not know what 'The Management Upstairs' had in mind for any of us, there was a stunned silence and an atmosphere that could be cut with a knife. I beat a hasty retreat before anything else could be said. Tom followed me post-haste as well!

Next morning, everyone decided to keep things low key and as pleasant as possible. The ceremony went without a hitch. Two good friends acted as witnesses. Other friends also attended and we repaired to a local pub for a celebration lunch. Poor Betty was awkward and stiff in young company, but to my great relief she behaved well – even if passing a few choice remarks as to the discrepancy between what should have been and what was. She and the carer left soon afterwards to start their return journey. A couple of hours later, we were at New Street railway station en route to our new life. Wearing a tailored clinging suit and high heels, I tapped my way along behind Tom who was weighed down with a suitcase. Walking along the platform, one of my rather high heels caught in a grid and the heel snapped. Not quite the image I was looking for! There was no time to dig out any other shoes, so I limped high/low, high/low onto the train.

On the journey, Tom suddenly became somewhat sullen and morose. When I asked him what was wrong, he told me his mother's home oppressed him and he was not looking forward to being there. Great! Just the boost I needed to my confidence! Arriving in time for supper, my heart sank. The neighbourhood was in a depressed suburb and the block of apartments looked like an entry to a prison block. His mother's flat was on the ground floor and dark. It had many heavy old pieces of furniture and lots of lace head-protectors on the sofa and chair. There was also a thick flowered tablecloth upon which what can only been described as a high tea had been prepared. Plants in old pots looked like something off a stage set. Tom settled himself in an armchair and said not a word. His mother and I did our best to get to know one another, but clearly this was not going to be a bed of roses for any of us!

My new mother-in-law seemed like a nice lady, but deeply sorrowful. Soon, she went to bed. There seemed to be no warmth between her and her son. This was a matter I brought up along with his silence after she left us on our own. He said it was our wedding night and we should go to bed. Everything would seem better in the morning. I desperately wanted that to be the case. So, feeling nervous but also excited, I went to bed.

We had not slept together before and to know his mother was in the next room did nothing to help me relax, although it did not seem to worry him. I knew beyond a shadow of a doubt I became pregnant that night. On sharing that information the next morning, I was scoffed at – but somehow I knew.

The next day, broken only by a walk outside, was not much better. Tom sat in the chair and said little. His mother and I tried to think of things to say to each other, but we did not do very well. Tom's sister

Liz and her husband Ben appeared towards evening. Liz was jolly and friendly and a nice evening followed. But they lived far away and were soon gone again. So life settled into a pattern that was disturbing to say the least. And I knew I was pregnant. I was imprisoned again and there seemed no escape. The saying 'out of the frying pan and into the fire' was a constant refrain in my head.

Six endless weeks later, it was confirmed. I was indeed pregnant. I was scared but excited, always having wanted a family more than anything else in life. Tom remained morose and appeared paranoid if I spoke to the milkman at the front door. His mother took it into her head I needed hot Marmite to drink at least three times a day. I hated Marmite and poured it into her many plants when she was out of the room! Hopefully they enjoyed it. It did not seem to kill them, at any rate. Tom was due to start his new job in Battersea and we found a shared attic flat in a mansion house block overlooking the park. There were a great many stairs, but at least we were to leave Morden. I was so glad to go, but still felt rather sorry for Tom's mother as we took our departure.

Before starting life in our new home, we took a short holiday. We went to a village in Dorset which meant a lot to Tom as he believed his father had been stationed there during the war. Called Litton Cheney, it turned out to be a profound déjà vu moment for me and meant nothing to him. I seemed to know that village historically and geographically. It was bizarre! I knew everything – where the pub was, where to park the car, where the walks were, where there was a hidden ruin – and I also knew I had never been there before in my life! Shrugging it off, I found it embarrassing that Tom paid it so much attention. That's just how it was with me. At least we were talking again!

Chapter 3 - The Light On The Landing

Thank goodness Tom cheered up a bit on leaving Morden and busied himself with getting used to his new job. I was expected to help out and so was included. I loved the bustle involved in the life of a political agent. Spending more time in the party rooms than Tom, I got to know all the people coming in and out and enjoyed their company. Even now, I did not think our relationship was all it should be, but I put this to the back of my mind on account of it being early days. Feeling well during pregnancy was a bonus and I walked for hours in Battersea Park talking to the baby inside me, the trees, the flowers and the earth. Asking the heavens to bless us all felt as natural as breathing.

A massive jumble sale had been arranged to raise funds and I was supposed to help with the work, but I pulled out. I thought I had really bad indigestion and went back to the flat to rest for a while. Not for long! Within the hour, I was in a taxi en route to hospital by myself. Not long afterwards, Tony was born. Weighing in at 6lb 12oz, he appeared to be on a mission to arrive in this world and nothing was going to stop him! Labour had taken sixteen hours, but for the first twelve I had no idea what was going on and was still under the impression I was suffering from terrible indigestion. When the second stage of labour started, I was left in no doubt. Tom was finally contacted and only appeared at the hospital when Tony was already nearly five hours old. Obviously, he was very tired and it seemed his interest in both me and the baby was more like duty than desire. In less than an hour he was gone again.

Jane's godmother, who was known as Auntie Molly, turned up at the hospital, bringing a cot blanket. She was a very kind and down-to-earth lady who gave me a talk about the just-had-a-baby-blues. She was most encouraging and, to this day, I am grateful for her blunt common sense and for telling me about the gulf between men's and women's emotional states following the birth of their first child. No one had ever told me anything like this before. It's all too easy for a woman to feel used or abandoned at these times. And that's just what I was – abandoned! Having no choice but to make baby Tony the priority for my love, Tom became jealous and demanding in ways I could not meet. Before long, he left our flat in Battersea where lack of money had reduced me to using the push-button light on the landing to feed the baby, and made tracks for his mother's house once more. As time passed, the situation could not go on. One evening, Tom informed me he had decided to leave Morden and commute to work from a friend's house. I was not told where this was located and I did not ask. Disappointed, disillusioned and a little bitter, I just let it be. He did not bother with either of us again. From now on, I was essentially a single mother.

I took Tony and moved in with a friend called Natalie and her baby, Symie, who lived in a block of flats next to Albert Bridge at the other end of Battersea Park Road. She had a good job as a Senior Market Research Manager. I got one too as a much more lowly Street Market Research Agent and we shared the cost of an au pair. This worked very well until, one day, I came home unexpectedly early to find the au pair standing at the bus stop wearing my best clothes and the children locked in the apartment! Furious would not be the word to describe how I felt. This would not do! I had to find better childcare than this. So I took a job in Hanbury, a village near Droitwich in Worcestershire, working for a farmer and his wife called Charles and Caroline. Their child, Leila, was the same age as Tony. Caroline and I would take it in turns to work one day with Charles and then spend the next day caring for both children. A happy year followed with lots of laughter. Before we went milking (something I had never done with one cow, let alone sixty) Charles insisted we should have a good shot of whisky. This was something else I wasn't used to. He swore it kept colds and flu at bay. I must say, in the year to come, none of us ever had any illness of any kind. Tony was now walking and talking, so I moved out of the farmhouse and lived in a luxury caravan a five-minute walk away. It was a wonderful time!

One year on, Charles and Caroline had to make some hard decisions as a result of farming restrictions, difficulties with their parents and a number of other problems. They decided they must sell up. It was all very sad and I don't know who was the more devastated, them or me. But we had to move on and make our respective plans. I needed a job fast so I advertised myself in the paper. The first line of the advert said: "Will anyone with a sense of humour employ me?" I went on to list a few trivial skills I had acquired and, to my amazement, I received 27 replies! I was called for five interviews and offered four jobs, two of which captured my interest. They were both in London. One was working for a small architect's practice in Knightsbridge. The other was a job with a PR firm and newspaper office in Fleet Street. I chose the latter. There was something about the boss, Tom H, and his wife Freda that appealed to me. Tom H grilled me like I had never been grilled before. He looked me straight in the eye and told me exactly what he wanted and was offering in return. A Lancastrian with a dour, stern manner and a great sense of humour that he rarely displayed, he turned out to be quite a taskmaster over the next few years. The firm handled a variety of PR clients and I was to be his assistant while Freda took care of the accounting side of the business. There were three other full-time people in the office – two typists and a lovely man called Bill. He was an elderly, tough ex-Navy man who still swayed as if on board ship when he walked. He moved requested newspaper articles around, delivered copy and handled the newspaper side. He was always very kind to me and made many cups of coffee to cheer me up during the years to come.

Now around two years old, Tony was minded by my friend Polly and her stamp-dealer husband Chris who lived in Wembley. They had two children themselves and Pol was at home full-time. Stamp-dealing was not doing very well in those days, so they were pleased to have some extra money coming in. Apart from the tiresome journey to and from the City, it proved a very satisfactory arrangement and Tony seemed to love it – so all was well.

Tom H was one tough cookie to work for. One of his sayings was: "Don't burn the midnight oil composing an epic." That was rich coming from a man who made me rewrite a piece on broiler chickens seventeen times before he was satisfied with the result!

Once, he sent me to a two-day Carpet Conference with a Yorkshire man and a Jewish man who shared a trade partnership in their carpet business. Apparently, they had both inherited their half from other people, so they had no choice but to become partners. They appeared to hate the sight of each other. I was instructed to write a piece about carpets, their business and their background and make it interesting!

"What can I write?" I asked in floods of tears when I spoke to Tom H by phone on the first evening. "You've sent me away with two people who bicker and fight their way through the day. No wonder potential customers walk straight by their business." Quietly, yet with great authority, he said to me: "Just find the confidence and the courage to handle it. That's why I pay you. Don't lose that account!" I did manage to write the piece, get the terrible two to behave and I didn't lose the account.

On occasions, Tom H was so taciturn that I thought he disliked me and regretted hiring me. Yet, when I had to have my tonsils out, he told me not to hurry back to work and also sent the biggest bunch of flowers I had ever seen. It was just before Christmas and Polly and the family had gone away to see relatives. So Tony and I were on our own for a while. I loved being with him and having the time to play, go for walks and just be domestic. I did a lot of heart searching during those few quiet days, feeling sad and lonely at no longer having a partner. I realised that we cannot control life nor manipulate circumstances to be the way we want. Things are just the way they are. Cuddling my lovely son, I sobbed long into the night – which did nothing for my unbearably sore throat!

A few days later, when a friend questioned whether I was the best person to look after Tony, I decided to stop feeling sorry for myself and to just get on with it as willingly and with as good a grace as I could muster. Returning to work, I was happy to be back in familiar circumstances and my colleagues seemed genuinely happy to see me again. Something had changed. I was definitely treated as a part of the 'A' team from that day on.

Chapter 4 - Town And Country

Polly was heavily pregnant with their third child and said, quite understandably, that she would no longer be able to look after Tony. Polly and Chris had a friend called Joe who was a lovable Irish rogue type. He rented a beautiful big house in Barnes, and with Tony now old enough for school, the commuting would be much easier for me from there than from Wembley. So we moved in. Joe proved utterly charming and so helpful – he just could not do enough for us. He asked me to marry him again and again...and eventually wore me down. I said 'yes'.

I was free to marry again, having finally parted company with Tom. The arrangement with his friend had not worked out, so he'd returned to living at his mother's once again. He spent his weekends visiting his sister and there he met and fell in love with a friend of hers. He wanted to marry her, so a quick and quiet divorce was obtained. This pleased everyone. We all moved on, somewhat relieved to be freed from what had been a mistake created by youth and inexperience on both sides.

After my engagement to Joe, two very strange things happened. Firstly, I was walking down the road one day and I felt a hand take mine. We walked along, hand in hand, with me staring down at my hand which looked as if it were being grasped by another – but there was no one visible there! It felt very strange, but was somehow hugely comforting. The second incident happened on the day of the wedding ceremony. Sitting in the car on the way there, I knew without a shadow of a doubt I should not be doing this. It was a kind of 'knowing' that filled my whole mind and body. My brain screamed 'NO!' It was as if I were standing outside of myself, looking in. The feeling was so overwhelming, I asked the driver to turn round and go to another town. He just laughed at me, saying it was typical pre-wedding nerves. I knew it wasn't! It was something else entirely, but I didn't have the necessary courage to kick up the fuss required to pull out at the last minute.

Did I pay for that mistake? Indeed, I did! The house in Barnes was large, so we rented out the excess rooms on a bed, breakfast and evening meal basis to a local school teaching English to foreign students. All the students (with one notable exception) were lovely in the two years we were doing it. Tony loved them and they spoiled him hugely with presents, play and attention. The students were good to me, too, and I enjoyed looking after them. However, still working in Fleet Street as well as cooking and cleaning for the students (up to eight in the house at the time) and looking after Tony who needed taking to school and fetching, I was getting very tired. Luckily, Tony loved his school and seemed immune to most childhood bugs, so he was rarely absent. Joe, however, was never in. Where he went and what he did were a mystery to me most of the time. That was until the day Tom H sent me home at lunchtime when we were quiet and he was concerned about me looking so tired.

Letting myself quietly into what should have been an empty house, I headed straight for our ground floor bedroom intending to lie down for an hour before fetching Tony from school. There was Joe and some girl having a high old time until I entered and interrupted them. Without a word, I turned on my heel and went to the kitchen to put the kettle on. I heard them leave. Running into the bedroom, I stripped the bed and put all the bedclothes in the washer. Then I turned the mattress, sprayed it and later remade the whole bed. Joe returned in the early hours drunk and was sensible enough to sleep on the sofa in the lounge.

On returning from work the following night, Joe waylaid me. I was so withdrawn, I think I was in danger of implosion! He talked and pleaded with me. "How many others?" I asked. "None!" he replied in a shocked tone. I just stood and looked at him. Eventually he told me there were several others and maybe I should get myself checked out for an STD. I didn't even know what that meant at the time. When I found out, I asked him to leave. I couldn't go. I had Tony and the students to think about and care for. The visit to the clinic was so shaming and still there was no relative to help me or share the problem with.

When the students found out Joe had gone, they were even nicer to me – especially two lads from Mexico called Marco and Carlos. We spent quite a few evenings drinking tea, watching TV and talking together. Tony loved them as they played with him endlessly. With these two and my friend Hettie who lived up the road, a year quickly passed and soon the students were leaving. Marco and Carlos later sent me an invitation to attend the forthcoming Olympic Games as their guest. If only! Affording the occasional taxi was a struggle, let alone the air fare to Mexico for Tony and me. That was out of the question. Still, it felt very nice to have been asked.

Next term, I went from the heaven of these two kind souls to the hell of their room replacement. She was a girl from France called Maria whom I knew was going to be trouble from the moment I set eyes on her. Not very clean, hair a mess, rude and surly, she demanded what she wanted and exactly when she wanted it. She complained about everything – the other students, a meal not being served on the dot of time, Tony making a noise...the list was endless. What a charmer! After putting up with her for a month, I phoned the school and asked if this girl could be found alternative accommodation. Enough was enough! Never having made a request like this before, it was complied with very quickly. Once she was gone, the bed and furniture had to be disposed of and the room fumigated.

We staggered on with Tony thriving and me exhausted. Work was still enjoyable and less difficult now I knew the ropes. Tom H and my colleagues were all very supportive. For a long while, I had known a man called Eddie who was very much older than me. He wrote for one of the trade papers specialising in mechanical engineering. A Yorkshire man with an easy relaxed manner, he treated me like a father and I lapped it up. Keen on health foods and fitness, he seemed to think it was his job to help me take better care of myself. One night after supper, and quite out of character for Eddie, we landed up in bed. Afterwards, I knew for the second time that I was pregnant. I told him this and he just said nonsense. I was on the pill and had never missed one, so it couldn't happen. But it did! A few weeks later, it was confirmed. Oh, Lord! What do we do now? Eddie said he had to go back to Saudi Arabia in eighteen months' time, come what may. Until that time, we would get a cottage together in the country. He would commute into town and I would take time off and enjoy being with Tony and the new baby.

Tom H was very lovely and said I could have my job back as soon as I wanted it. In the meantime, he would have to get someone else in. He gave me a truly affectionate send off and I was really touched. We moved to a remote country cottage three miles outside Heathfield in Sussex. It was an end cottage in a row of three farm cottages and it suited us just fine. A very happy time followed. Tony loved the country and climbed trees, played in barns, rode go-carts and generally had a ball. A family with two children lived at the other end of the row of cottages, so he was never short of playmates either. Life became gentle for once. Bill, the owner of the farm, was really kind. So was his wife Esther who was so thoughtful it was almost overwhelming. I put her up for a neighbour-of-the-year award and she won it! She was tickled pink when she was interviewed by a reporter and photographed for a top London magazine.

Huge, but healthy and regaining a sense of perspective, I knew having this baby would be a different ball game from Tony. There seemed to be a level of understanding between me and the baby already – something like a telepathic communication between us. It was like a 'knowing', an understanding of what was needed to promote our mutual well-being. One evening, Tony was staying overnight with his friends next-door-but-one and so Eddie and I decided to go to the movies to see Oh! What A Lovely War in Uckfield. I was uncomfortable and restless through the film. In the foyer afterwards, just as Eddie said he would go and get the car, my waters broke. The baby was on the way! After rushing me to hospital, Eddie returned home to ensure adequate arrangements were in place for Tony.

Jackie was born a few hours later, a beautiful and healthy baby girl. I was back home with her within 48 hours. I arrived to find my wonderful neighbour doing the washing and ironing so that I wouldn't feel burdened down by it. Tony had just turned seven and once he had got over his initial jealousy of the new arrival, he loved his baby sister dearly. She turned out to be placid and friendly. So a wonderful six months followed. The only blot on the landscape during this idyllic time came from a car crash we had one Sunday lunchtime. We were driving down a narrow country lane when another car came careering towards us. Eddie, who was driving, had nowhere to go and so we were hit head on. Tony broke two ribs, my legs were badly cut and Eddie had a couple of nasty bruises. Mercifully, the baby was just fine. The police and an ambulance crew were on the scene very quickly. They were very helpful to me and the children, but not so kind to the other driver who was also hurt. He was told he was not priority and would have to wait when we reached the hospital. I almost felt sorry for the young man. He was obviously in pain and terrified what his parents would say when they found out he'd crashed the car.

Eddie dropped a bombshell on us one weekend. He said we must move back to London because, in another few months, he would be going to Saudi Arabia. He wanted to be sure I was in a position to go back to work and get the family settled and comfortable before his departure. Sadly leaving our little haven in East Sussex, we moved a few weeks later to a spacious mansion flat in Chiswick. After much hard work, the flat looked great and proved very comfortable. Tony was enrolled into his first 'proper' school, a seventeen-year-old girl called Chrissie who needed a home was coming from Middlesborough to work for us, and I got my old job back. Tom H had landed the account of a big car-hire company launching in the UK in a few months time, so he was really pleased to hear I wanted to return to work.

Chrissie proved a sheer good-humoured joy! On her first day, I told her the porter would ring a bell and she was to put the rubbish into the lift outside the kitchen window. I forgot to say leave it in the bin! She gaily complied and tipped the whole lot all over the porter's head! He met me on my way home looking very grim faced, but later he saw the funny side of it. Then Eddie left. I really couldn't understand why he was going, but couldn't argue because he'd said from the start that was how it was going to be. He was doing the rounds of his relatives prior to going, so would still be in the UK for another month, and would call prior to leaving. Chrissie loved the kids and they loved her in return. Also, I was just about making enough money, so we could manage.

Much to my surprise, Betty paid us a visit with her carer. She was in London seeing a specialist and thought she would like to come and see us. Letters and phone calls had been the order of the day up to this point, so seeing her in person came as something of a shock. She treated the kids like interesting specimens who should be observed from afar but not touched in case they had an infection. It annoyed me intensely, but I had to bite my tongue as she left a cheque for a hundred pounds on her departure. That was manna for me just then.

Chapter 5 - Natural Sensitive

So we were okay and life was good. We all had a home that we liked. I loved the kids and they appeared well and content. Chrissie also loved them. We all had friends. So it came as something of a surprise when two strange incidents occurred which left everyone feeling totally mystified.

The first occurred when a friend called June called round with her baby, Scott, who was about the same age as Jackie. We put them both in Jackie's cot, end-to-end, for a nap. Later, Tony called me in a panic. He had gone in to see if they were awake and the whole room was covered in faeces, even though it was way out of their reach! This was scary! We checked the babies and found they were fine, so nothing untoward seemed amiss. I had no choice but to set to with a bucket of water and some disinfectant, scrubbing the whole room – cot, carpet and all. We never did find out the whys and wherefores of that weird and very unpleasant incident.

On another occasion, some other friends were round including two brothers called David and Michael with their current girlfriends. Huge imposing chaps, they were. David went to the bathroom and came rushing back to find Michael.

"Just come and listen to this!" exclaimed David. After about five minutes, they both returned to me and said: "Do you know your baby dreams in colloquial Russian?" "Don't be silly," I replied. "Surely she's just muttering!" So we all went and listened again. Would you believe it? It was true! David and Michael were White Russians who had only lived in London for ten years and had spent all their formative years in Russia. So they could understand what she was saying in her sleep. Jackie talked about the sort of difficulties people faced when crops did not grow well in the country, saying it was hardly worth the effort to get into town to sell them. She was really complaining about others around her who she thought were not pulling their weight in the manner she thought they should. She was quite cross with them! Where she had learned to speak in everyday Russian was a complete mystery to all of us. Like the earlier cot incident, I cannot to this day find any rational explanation for such an unusual and baffling phenomenon.

A couple of years passed and Tom H asked me if I would be willing to work for a few months as an 'insider' for the rent-a-car company about to launch. This was the same car-hire company whose launch had been proposed two years earlier, but there had been big problems with the choice of outlet sites. These had now been resolved by taking out a franchise to place their offices in big hotels. As many of the existing staff were Americans who were not familiar with British culture, it was suggested that I should actually work as if I were a member of the car-hire staff. There were many things that I needed to know and learn.

The first office was located in a hotel just beside Heathrow Airport. The other was in Central London, working out of a busy hotel in Piccadilly. I would divide my time between the two. While working at Heathrow, I could take any car available home at night. When in London, I would continue to commute. Well, a change being as good as a rest, I said yes to this job and for the next few months that was the way it was.

I learned a lot. When people do not return a rental car, it is called a conversion and the police become involved. They check the paperwork and then invite the person who hired out the car down to Scotland Yard to look at mug shots. This was exciting the first few times, but became time consuming and not nearly so interesting after that. And talk about expecting the unexpected! The only person who was ever banned from hiring a car while I was there was an airline pilot who drank so much he kept smashing up our vehicles! He used to take neat oxygen to sober up before flying. Eventually, he got found out and was fired.

During this time, not only did I learn about car-hire, but also about the daily life in a central city hotel. Petty theft from rooms, the propositioning of the security staff when they investigated, the antics of the guests and the comings and goings of the high-class (and wildly expensive) prostitutes who worked the hotel – these were all regular occurrences. The prostitutes fascinated me. There were only a few of them and they had an arrangement with the porters and the security staff. The girls paid a commission and everyone turned a blind eye.

What an innocent I was! I had no idea what was going on. Then, one day, one of the girls told me her husband had died recently and she needed to keep her three children at the expensive private schools they were attending for another few years. She wore a business suit, carried a briefcase and only worked nine-to-five, so no one would find out what she was doing. She made a lot of money and I believed her when she said she would quit as soon as she could. I don't know what I expected a call-girl to be like, but it wasn't such an ordinary, well-dressed person like this with subtle make-up and a quiet, well-educated voice.

One day, working in this location, I was checking for conversions and my colleague Pat was working the desk. She called me over and said a couple of handsome hunks had just walked in and were coming towards us. I looked up with interest. I was free and single again. David, one of the Russian brothers, was a solicitor and had arranged a divorce from Joe post-haste when he found out what had been going on. Joe had made no protest and was all too keen to hush the situation up. I felt really sad about parting from Eddie. Not only did we share a daughter, but we had been really good friends. I never heard a word from him – either from direct contact at home or gossip at work.

"Leave the one on the left alone," I said. "I'm going to marry him." "How can you possibly know that?" asked Pat. "I don't know. I just do," I replied.

This conversation with Pat got me thinking. Do other people just know stuff intuitively like I do? If not, why not? There was nothing special or different about me. Maybe I was nuts! Should I dare to find out? All my life, having wanted to be acceptable and accepted, did I have the courage to question this unusual ability of mine? What if I didn't like the answer? Supposing it was some kind of strange mental state for which I would need to have prolonged treatment? I couldn't really risk that as it would mean being separated from my beloved children.

Once, when taking one of the children for a check-up, I did casually mention to my GP that I had 'a friend' who was able to do that sort of thing. He just said my friend needed to talk to a priest not a doctor. It sounded as if this person was a natural sensitive. What did that mean? The only priest I knew well enough to talk to about such matters was Guy who had now been elevated to being a Bishop. So I was not about to tell him! Betty had often said he thought my antics to be outrageous. Actually, I was none too thrilled with hers, either, but

I'd learned enough by now to keep my mouth shut about them and allow it all to be one-way traffic. So I'd always left any discussion about my undoubted psychic gifts on the back-burner until the right opportunity to reveal it should arrive.

It seemed like ages until Ray asked me out. He and his friend Brian were moonlighting from their day jobs and helping out with the hotel security. Their office was located behind our allocated hotel space for the car-hire company and they took to talking to us when there was a lull at work. We all got to know each other well. My friend Pat and Brian got quite close and, one day, she told him what I had said. Naturally, he told Ray and they were so curious about my knowledge of the future that they tackled me about it. Both of them had previous experience of psychic powers. Brian had once worked as a prison officer and regaled us with stories of people in prison who experienced paranoid delusions or heard voices. Ray had a mother and an aunt who had personal knowledge of psychic occurrences. But, even so, the pair of them made light of my abilities and were inclined to mock me about them. So, initially, I tended to give them a wide berth and withdrew as much as possible into myself. I was also none too pleased with Pat's betrayal of my confidence and her predisposition to gossip. So I tried to keep my distance from her, too. Tom H laughed when I told him my problems and said my unusual intuition was a huge asset and a part of the reason he had employed me in the first place. He reckoned all the dramatic happenings in my past had made me a little oversensitive. Coupled with my desire to love and be loved, I was becoming too self-conscious about my life. His advice was that I should just get on with it!

So Ray and I started our arduous courtship, he eventually discovering what I'd known right from the start. He met and liked the children and became a regular visitor at the house. He had been married before and had two children, but he didn't see them for reasons I never fully understood. He seemed to take to my two and accepted them as his own. Tony seemed none too pleased and was forgivably jealous, just as he had been when his sister was born. Perhaps he would accept it better with time. I met Ray's parents and loved them immediately, just as I loved their son. His father, Pa (as he was known to one and all), was a tough Londoner who'd got a job post-war as a newspaper seller where St Paul's joins Fleet Street. He worked until he was in his mid-eighties. Everyone in the area knew and loved him. He was like an institution, giving advice, information and comfort to everyone who came to know him. He smoked untipped cigarettes at the rate of about 60-a-day. Once, when he was giving me a lift in his car, he dropped a lit cigarette between his legs and stopped all the traffic as he tried to find it. I was reduced to helpless laughter. Then he told me he loved me and thought I was just what his son needed.

He promised me all the help he could give. Crying now, I thanked him from the bottom of my heart. His wife Gill, my mother-in-law-to-be, also made me most welcome, talking to me about anything and everything and including me in all their family matters. This was a novel and welcome experience indeed! Ray's sister Molly was a scream and had a wicked temper on her. She and her family lived in Kent, next door to a respected local doctor. When she lost her temper, she used to shout and swear like a trooper. Her embarrassed husband and two children had to rush around closing all of the windows. Then she would follow, opening them all again!

Ray and I really loved each other and life felt very good indeed. He moved into my house in Chiswick. As he was out at work all day like me, the necessary adjustments were minimal. Finally, it seemed as if things were settled...but it was not to be. After a very happy couple of years, Chrissie decided she was going to go back to Middlesborough to live. She said she wanted to settle down and marry a local lad and did not want her future to be in London. At about the same time, Ray was made redundant. Rather than trying to find similar work, he decided he'd also like to leave London and run a country pub. He could not or would not begin to understand why I was not keen. Loving my job and my home, I didn't want to go anywhere! It seemed everyone was free to do what they wanted, except me! But I loved Ray above everything else and needed to be with him, so I had no choice but to give in. It upset me greatly to give my notice to Tom H, the man who'd been so loyal and supportive to me through all the years. He was gracious as always and understood why I had to leave. So, in spite of my reluctance, things proceeded apace. Ray had several interviews with various breweries that were offering jobs in the west of England. He rented a house in Montgomery for a period of three months, the idea being he should go down there with Chrissie and the children (Chrissie having agreed to stay on until my notice was worked). I would join them at weekends, though I was not keen on this idea. I had never ever been apart from the children, but there was little I could do but agree.

The day came for their departure and off they went. Staying in a friend's spare room, I continued to work out my notice. Tom H was as encouraging as ever, but this time it took more than one of Bill's coffees to cheer me up. My first weekend visit felt like I was a foreigner in someone else's life, although I was thrilled to be with the children again and they were to be with me. We walked, talked, laughed, looked at horses, grass, trees and dogs. All too soon, I was off back to London, but left all of them with a lighter heart seeing how much the children were enjoying the countryside and how well they were being looked after by Chrissie. She had proved so very loving and capable during the time she'd been working as a nanny. I was going to miss her terribly. Eventually, Ray got a job in a pub in Ironbridge on the boundary between Shropshire and Wales. He was to start immediately, so I joined my family and Chrissie finally left to return to the North.

After a rousing but tearful send-off from my colleagues at work, I left the house in Chiswick and caught the train to start a new chapter in my life. Not long after I arrived, my adventurous daughter tried to climb up onto the seat of a tractor that was parked at the end of the garden. She didn't make it and fell between the engine and the mudguard, badly cutting her face. The hospital could not stitch it as it was too close to her eye, so they used butterfly strips instead. During the night, I looked in on her to find her cot resembling a bloody, post-battle scene! Stitches were obviously required. They were duly put in and then had to be taken out again because it was discovered she'd also pierced her tear duct. There was no choice but to leave the wound alone and hope it would heal naturally. The next four days were a messy and worrying time, but the resilience of youth saw Jackie through and soon all was well – although she still bears the scar to this day. It was the first time (but by no means the last) that one of the children hurt themselves in their new and exciting environment. What with this trauma, leaving work and losing Chrissie's help, I was somewhat distraught. Ray couldn't understand it. He was far too excited about his new job as a pub manager.

Chapter 6 - Phantoms and Voices

It seemed a little ironic that I was being asked to make a new life in a place called Ironbridge. I was certainly being called upon to have great tensile strength and learning how to be flexible enough to pursue a whole new lifestyle. The hours were so challenging! The police from two districts met up regularly in our pub. There was also an iron foundry nearby, so the night shift would be banging on the door early in the morning knowing I would be up getting the children ready for school. Then there were the late nights as well. This was more tiring than being pregnant! Always being in a rush to meet the discipline of opening hours, turning up at school smelling of beer, going to the cash-and-carry at the weekends — it was a tough life! I was also very aware that living in a pub was not really appropriate for children. Yet they appeared to be quite enjoying themselves and Jackie became something of a mascot for the teams playing darts, dominoes and football from the pub. People were always buying her crisps and I was always taking them off her! With Ray's supervision, Tony took to shooting with an air rifle. He fired at anything they could think of like baubles on the Christmas tree, pegs on the washing line, cigarette packets on the wall. This was something that absolutely infuriated me, but appeared to amuse them hugely!

Suddenly, and with no warning, I was pregnant again. Why was it that birth control just did not seem to work for me? The doctor's comment was the only thing that might work was an aspirin between the knees! More tired with this pregnancy than at any time before, I began to notice that Ray spent a lot of time on the wrong side of the bar or out with the various teams attached to the pub. As I was besotted with him and he was a very charismatic character, I forgave him every time, even when a customer had to change a barrel for me when he wasn't there. Ray had decided he wanted to become a pub tenant rather than a manager and was in discussions about this with the brewery already.

As I was too pregnant and too tired to go with him, Ray went off looking at possible tenancies by himself. He came back one day to say he had found the one. We arranged to visit it again so I could take a look as well, but circumstances prevented it. Tony was away from school with some virulent bug and could not be left. Nor could I risk Jackie going down with it, let alone myself. So negotiations went ahead and arrangements were made without my involvement. Now almost eight months pregnant with two children and a dog, it was time to move again. Having packed up all our stuff, we arrived at our new home in Bishop's Castle just over the Welsh border shortly after Ray who had gone on ahead to meet a representative of the brewery. Taking one look at the building, I detected an atmosphere that reeked of history – but, according to my sensory network, the history was not good! There was a feeling of hostility that surrounded the building, hanging over the whole village with the pub at the centre of it like a dark cloud. The place was deceptive. Its historical legacy made it appear very attractive, but I thought otherwise. What was going on here? I just could not fully understand it.

Putting on as cheerful a face as I could muster, I went inside and – oh my goodness – it was even worse! The interior of the pub was even more oppressive and heavy than outside. It appeared to be a no-women zone. Everyone in the pub was male, most of them looking as old, decrepit and gnarled as the wood in the bar. No one seemed to notice the negative atmosphere or the absence of good cheer but me. In fact, everyone in the family appeared intrigued by the locals except me. Eventually, one of them spoke to me in a strong Welsh accent, telling me that the last three landlords had all died on the premises, but the women were left alone. Great! Just what I needed to hear, especially as there were no women in sight. The regulars quizzed us about our background and appeared pleased we were a family, this being a small market town where families were valued. One old boy told us to be careful what we did with the pub and to make sure the men were looked after. Furious and muttering about male chauvinist pigs, I went through to our small family lounge to see what I could do to make it appear a home.

Having had a look around upstairs, I asked Tony what he thought of the place. "Spooky!" he said. "No, just old," I replied, but somewhere deep within me I agreed with his verdict.

He went off to explore the large garden which was to prove a haven for the children and Mutley, the new dog Ray had bought to keep our old dog Glen company. The kitchen was light and airy and my favourite room by far. Built as an extension, it served both the family and the pub. It was just as well that I liked the kitchen as I was to spend many hours in there, providing bar food and snacks at lunchtime. The bedrooms were old, creaky and full of dark beams, but they seemed a lot more cheerful when they had our own possessions in them. The two bars remained exactly the same, Ray having bought all the fixtures and fittings from the previous landlord. The tables and chairs were old and rustic while the carpet and the curtains looked none too clean or bright. It felt dirty, even though the cleaners had worked hard to keep it up to a good standard. They could do nothing with it.

Too pregnant to do anything but look after the children, I waddled in and out of the bar, working very little. This meant Ray was super-busy and it became a joke that I had better not give birth on market day as that was the busiest day of the week and pubs could not close at all on that day. Well, of course, that was the very day I went into labour! The doors were closed just long enough for Ray to drive me to a tiny little hospital in the next village. Tony and Jackie were at school, so as soon as he'd handed me over, he rushed back to reopen the pub and make arrangements for the children to be collected. Thinking this birth would be quick and easy as it was my third time, I was perfectly happy with this arrangement. It seemed to be in the best interests of all. Nearly thirty hours later, I was beside myself with pain and distress. The staff called the local doctor and he and the three ward staff did everything in their power to help me. I cannot tell you how many enemas were given as I lay and watched their stocks in their tiny delivery room dwindle to nothing. They told me I was now too ill to be moved and couldn't be sent to a much bigger hospital thirty miles away, so we just waited some more. Four hours later, this tiny bundle arrived. She weighed less than 5 lbs. I couldn't understand how it had been so very difficult when she was so small and quite unfinished with no eyebrows, nails or hair. She was promptly wrapped in lint and cotton wool, then in tin foil to keep her warm, and placed in an incubator. Neither of us were going home quickly this time! We had not picked a name for her yet, so she was nicknamed 'Soapy' due to the number of enemas that had been given during labour.

By the time we did go home, Soapy had become Heather. We

were welcomed warmly by one and all. A routine began to establish itself and, once again, I hoped for an easy and straightforward time that didn't happen! Strange things began to occur for which there was no obvious explanation. At night, Ray and I would clearly hear footsteps overhead, but on going upstairs there was no one moving about. Both the older children were always asleep in bed and the baby was downstairs with us. Then things began to get lost or seemed to have been moved. Worst of all, so many accidents occurred that the local doctors started saying who has 'the Missus' brought in now? Tony tripped over in the car park, requiring stitches from elbow to wrist. Only a week before, he had cut his leg by falling on some glass almost in the same place. Then an electrician who was mending the external pub sign had forgotten to take his wedding ring off and had hammered it flat on his finger. He was almost as worried about how it had happened as he was about the extensive injury. He told me, while we were waiting for him to be seen by a doctor that his left hand had been on one side of the ladder and his right hand holding the hammer had been on the other. So how had he managed to hit himself? He had no idea. It was a complete mystery!

Often, the dogs barked at nothing when in their kennel in the garden. I asked the kids if they noticed this and were relieved to get out of the house to go to school. They said no. But I was mighty relieved to go shopping after I dropped them off, for sure. One day I was in the kitchen getting the lunchtime food under way when Ray staggered in, as white as a sheet, with half his face shaved and the other half covered in shaving foam. He said he had just seen a cloudy type substance lying on the floor under the wash hand basin. Normally a highly rational man, he was clearly shaken to the core. He sat at the kitchen table, trembling, while I made him a cup of tea. Afterwards, he was very reluctant to go back to the bathroom. So we both went together, but the bathroom appeared to be as usual.

During the lunchtime session, Ray quizzed the locals about the supernatural history of the building. He was told that all the previous landlords, for as long as the punters could remember, had died in the pub. The woman always remained untouched. It was just the men who suffered. The previous landlord had died where he stood at the basin in the bathroom. One minute, he was apparently perfectly healthy. The next, he was dead. Immediately, Ray got onto the brewery, very cross he had been told none of this before. On and on went the stories of death and disaster. After all these supernatural happenings, we were beginning to get spooked and Ray's conversations with the brewery became more and more intense. Not willing to risk our lovely little family, we gave notice to the brewery and they said they would do all they could to facilitate our departure as quickly as possible. Six months and several more incidents later, we were desperate to move on. By now, I couldn't care less that we had paid for all the fixtures and fittings in the bar. I wanted out! To my surprise, so did Ray. He told the brewery that we would be leaving after closing time on Saturday in three weeks time. On Sunday, the pub would be closed and he would not be there to open up on Monday morning.

On the Sunday morning three weeks later, we left in a Transit van and a car. We headed for Devon. Betty had been saying we were selfish for not visiting her when she was nearing the end of her life, so we decided to take a holiday, see her and decide what we should do next. We hired a six-berth caravan on a site where each van had a third of an acre before another one was sited. High on a cliff top, it was not long until we all began to recover from the traumas of our previous life. Despite it still being February, we took long walks on the cliff tops and the beach which the children loved. We cooked and ate leisurely meals and we slept and played. It was bliss! After a few weeks, two major things happened in quick succession. Ray was asked by an acquaintance of his called Bill if he would be willing to strip and sell pine for his thriving antique and second-hand furniture business. He agreed immediately. Meanwhile, I was asked by the people running the caravan site if I would stay on for the forthcoming season, seeing people in and out and cleaning the vans between guests. This was ideal because the work could all be managed around the children. So we were set to stay in Devon. This pleased me because it would give time to see what was going to happen regarding Betty whose health had taken a downturn recently.

This proved to be a happy season indeed. Tony and Jackie were settled in schools they both liked and baby Heather came everywhere with me. We also got on like a house on fire with the family who owned the site and had many suppers together in their lovely old farmhouse. Ray loved the work he was doing and we all saw much more of each other than we had done when we lived in the pub. The summer seemed to fly by. As the season came to a close, it became rather cold, especially as we had to put Heather's pram outside if we wanted to cook a meal so she wouldn't be affected by the calor gas fumes. So we decided to take the opportunity to rent a cottage in the next village. That village was Sidbury. So I found myself back in a place that I had been to before.

Ray was doing really well in his new job and I was busy with the children and Betty. She had to be moved from one care home to another that offered more in the way of nursing care. It also turned out to be a much nicer home. Being close to Sidbury, I used to drop in a few times a week while she was settling in, sometimes taking one or two of the children. She remained hugely self-absorbed and critical of everyone, especially me. But I now had children, I had more confidence and was much better at dealing with her. The staff at the new home were younger and had families themselves, making the atmosphere much happier altogether. We unkindly named these visits 'the death run' as, every time Betty wanted a visit, she phoned and said she was dying. We were to be hoisted by our own petard as the death run was to last for another ten years!

Life went on at a relatively gentle pace until one fateful night a couple of years later. Ray went out one evening to have a drink with some guys from work, saying he would not be more than a couple of hours. The children and I had a nice evening playing games and watching a bit of television. Once they were all in bed, it was wonderful – a rare hour to contemplate, read and listen to the quiet! Time went by. I tried to phone the number Ray had left me, but to no avail. I thought he had got into a bit of a session and decided to go to bed. After a shower, the phone rang. It was the hospital to say Ray was to spend the night there following an accident. They were not very forthcoming, but as it turned out, it did not matter. Soon there was a knock on the door. It was the police who told me that Ray had been involved in a case of mistaken identity. He had been leaving the pub hours earlier on his way home when a man had hit him on the head from behind with a car jack. As it was a head injury, he was being kept in overnight.

The following few weeks were a nightmare. The worst thing was trying to keep the children quiet. Ray had to go to the police station and have the injuries photographed and he was popping pills to try to get his headaches under control. Understandably, he was on a very short fuse and his temper flared at the slightest thing. So the children and I got very fit as we walked the lanes to try to give him some space and some quiet time. After a few weeks, things improved, but not hugely. Eventually, he decided to dissolve his partnership with Bill and travel round Wales with another friend called Les, trying to locate

Welsh dressers to do up and sell. It was a relief to wave them off and not to live on tenterhooks for a while. Not for long, though. Three weeks later, the phone rang. Ray and Les had decided they could make a go of things in Wales, so a house had been rented for us with workshop space outside. The children and I were expected to join them in two weeks' time. I was told that gave me plenty of time to pack up the cottage and make the journey north!

I was not a happy bunny, but I did what I was asked. I went to see the landlord who was so kind and caring, releasing us from our tenancy of the cottage immediately. Betty was not very happy that I was leaving, but now being settled, she took the news well enough. Breaking the news to the children was a lot easier than I had anticipated. They helped with the packing and looked upon our latest move as a big adventure. The day arrived for us to depart. The old Transit was packed to the roof – children in, plus dogs – and off we went. About two hours later, I realised we'd left Tony's goldfish on the window ledge, something I did not live down for many a year to come. Travel was slow and the weather was not good. We got as far as the Road Bridge over the Severn when we broke down, fortunately near a service station. The mechanics were not keen on the dogs, so these had to be tied up at the back of the garage while the children and I went for a welcome food break. Four hours later, having spent nearly all the cash I had with me, we set off again. Nervous that we would not arrive before dark, we pushed on as fast as the ageing van would go. Having used a whole tank of petrol, we tried to find a garage that was open which was not easy. Wales was very different from the south west of England and we had to go out of our way to fill up one last time. It was now pouring with rain. We all wondered just where we were going. It seemed to become more and more wild and remote. Eventually, when we got to Bala Lake, the windscreen wipers failed. Tony and I had to reach out of the side windows and wipe the screen manually as best we could. Finally, around eleven p.m., we arrived. We pulled into the driveway and there was Ray waiting for us. He took over the children, the dogs and the unloading. I just fell on a bed fully-clothed and remembered nothing until the next morning. Presumably Ray had covered me with a duvet.

Having checked everyone was still asleep, I crept downstairs to take a look around. I wasn't thrilled with what I saw. The cold, grey slate floors felt dampish even on a fine morning and the square room sizes were rather depressing. There was one room to the right of the front door and one to the left with the kitchen at the back. The stairs were right opposite the front door. Feng Shui had not become the popular notion it is today, but I sensed the position of these stairs made everything feel awkward and uncomfortable. In modern terms, they 'let the abundance out'. Also, outside, it was raining, so the views held no massive appeal either! But it was no use crying over spilt milk. We were here now and that's how it was going to stay. It was time to cheer things up by making a big family breakfast. Then we could all go for a walk and explore the area.

Unbeknown to me, the dresser business was not going well for Ray and Les and they were getting into debt. I noticed the money I had saved from working at the caravan site was dwindling fast but, as the boys went out most days and always came home very up-beat, I did not realise how bad things really were. To make matters worse, a terrible incident occurred a few months later when our dog Glen chased some sheep and the farmer shot him. I began to understand that the Welsh were not that keen on the English. I had already upset them by wearing trousers, going into the pub to get Ray some cigarettes by myself and hanging nappies on the line on Sundays! I really began to find out that the values of others differed considerably. A farmhouse on the other side of the road became vacant to rent, so we moved in. It was a warmer and much friendlier house and the farmer still had animals in a barn which the children enjoyed. Open fireplaces meant that wood had to be cut as a priority each morning. Tony and I learned to use a double-handed saw. Jackie helped to collect the wood and the three of us spent many happy hours together. When the wood was in for the day, we went to see how the animals were getting on. Then it was back to the kitchen Aga to warm ourselves up.

Tony managed to pull a bedroom door handle off, locking himself and Jackie inside. This caused great consternation for an hour or so, after which we managed to open the door. Tony also started to walk into the village to get milk, but one day I caught him hitchhiking back. This frightened me and, in turn, I frightened him with my lecture on the dangers this involved. I was beginning to understand that being a parent meant really doing the best you could for your children and that, sometimes, 'tough love' had to be deployed. This seemed heartless and unkind, but now some discipline had to be observed. It couldn't just be cuddles anymore.

Ray's parents paid us a welcome visit. Being out-and-out Londoners, they were not impressed by the current set-up, supporting me and the children and being really tough on Ray. He didn't appreciate this at all. I loved my parents-in-law and was so touched when they took both the children out and bought them new shoes. Pa and Gill were not well off themselves and it was such a kindness. After two weeks, they left. I was sad; Ray was relieved. Then worrying things began to happen. People started coming to the farm, looking for Ray. To begin with, I thought they were customers looking for furniture. Only later did I discover they were debt-collectors. Ray told me to tell them he was not in, whether he was or not. I was still besotted with him, so I did as he asked. One day, I watched with dread as a suited man drove up to the farm – only to have him tell me he was the rat man from the Ministry! Was this a joke? No, he really was! A new strain of rat was making its way across the county and farms were their prime location. This man was tracing how far they had got. I thought it was the funniest thing that he was wearing a pin stripe suit, black shoes and looked way too smart to be doing the job he was employed to do. Eventually, Ray sold his stock of Welsh dressers and managed to clear his most pressing debts. This brought us some relief from the callers. I was never privy to what exactly went on financially, but as far as I was concerned, at least life was quieter now.

The farm on which we were living turned out to be built on the site of an old Roman settlement. We found this out after both Tony and I saw what appeared to be an elderly Centurion walking across the boundary at the back of the house. I knew when he was about as I heard his armour clanking as well as seeing him. We named him Claudius. He was not hostile in any manner, shape or form. In fact, we saw him so much that he began to feel like a friend. Researching the history of the house, it turned out that the field behind us was the site of a food store for the nearby Roman army encampment and it was guarded day and night to prevent anything being stolen. Looking back, it seemed strange how easily we accepted his ghostly presence. Two Australian girls came to stay with us for a week and one of them saw him, too. She was freaked out for days!

Mercifully, Ray found himself some new work. He had been a paramedic in the Navy for some years, so got a job as a District Officer for the Red Cross. His brief was to make sure people were cared for properly and transported safely to hospital from areas in which medical facilities had not yet been built. His first appointment was to be in Skelmersdale, a new overspill town for Liverpool. Well, I thought, this had to be better than rural Wales, especially as I found out I was pregnant again. Ray was so thrilled at getting another chance at a family, he decided we should be married. His brother Brian also lived in Skem (as it was commonly known) with his wife, Wendy. Brian and Ray arranged all the wedding details between them. On the day itself, Brian came over and we had a very quiet ceremony with him and the children attending. Wendy was unable to come as she was ill. Then we packed up all our stuff and moved to a new maisonette provided by the Red Cross. This two-floored, upstairs flat had three bedrooms and a huge living room, plus the usual kitchen and bathroom. It was warm, manageable and so much smaller than the previous farmhouse. We all liked it. To my relief, Tony made friends quickly and became a talented mimic of the local Scouse accent. He adjusted brilliantly to yet another change, settling in well and becoming an avid Air Cadet attending an after-school class each week.

Jackie, Heather and I enjoyed visiting Wendy, the girls being keen to try her favourite dish which turned out to be a tin of chicken soup poured over a bowl of chips! Being early on in pregnancy, I had to go out and look round the garden as this local delicacy made me feel distinctly queasy! They thought this was a scream. Certainly, my memories of life in Skem involve a lot of humour. One day, a man talking to me at a bus stop told me I was a brave lass with an adventurous spirit having come all the way up here from London. It turned out he had been no further than Wigan, the next town, all his life! On another occasion, very early in the morning, I drove Ray to work as I needed the car. On the way back, I was stopped by a police road check. Just wearing my pyjamas, a dressing gown and slippers, I felt very exposed and vulnerable. The cops thought it was hilarious and no doubt I was the topic of conversation in the canteen that day! After that experience, I never ever put myself in that position again.

Heather was now four and had started school, so the inevitable round of childhood illnesses began. I had covered a large settee with some dusky pink velvet curtains I had been given and it seemed that the girls spent weeks on either end of it with chicken pox, quickly following a severe dose of whooping cough. As soon as Ray came in, I hurried out to the local launderette in an effort to keep up with the washing and drying of bedding. We also got introduced to nits. These were a constant battle, both the girls having shoulder-length hair. A family down the road had their heads shaved and iodine painted on them, something I had never come across before. Even though I insisted on ponytails, we still had to monitor the situation with care.

Tony seemed to escape the illnesses and the nits, spending his time making model aeroplanes which hung from the ceiling in his bedroom like an air show. One weekend, to give everyone a much needed change, we all went to visit Molly and George in Kent. We all felt very exited as we piled into the car. We had an estate in those days and placed a mattress in the back for the children to sleep on because we were setting off very early in the morning. We had no idea there was anything dangerous about this as it was before the era of compulsory seat belts. Arriving in time for breakfast, the children met their two cousins, Bill and Betsy, who literally took them over. They loved having the opportunity to play with and care for children younger than themselves. It was chaotic, noisy and fun!

Warm hearted and loving as ever, Molly decided she was going to dye my hair. I was now 32 and my hair had been going white since I was 26. As I'd had black hair before, she dyed it black...and it looked just awful! I resembled Morticia from The Addams Family on TV! From that day to this, it has never been dyed again. It was a lovely weekend and was over all too soon. Measles was the next thing on the horizon and, once again, the pink sofa was put to good use. Heather recovered completely, but Jackie continued to experience bad headaches and kept being sick. I was not happy about this, so I decided to really hassle the local GP. As a result, she was soon taken to our nearest hospital in Ormskirk by ambulance. They could not seem to find out what was wrong with her. Despite blood tests and a lumbar puncture, she got sicker and sicker. Eventually, bacterial meningitis was diagnosed and she was moved into a private side room off the children's ward. She became seriously ill. Her temperature went up and up and she was placed on an ice-bed with fans going. For five weeks, she remained in a coma and it was touch and go. Time seemed to play tricks on me then. Nothing ever seemed to happen, yet there was a lot of activity going on at the same time.

For probably the first time in my life, I understood the meaning of true prayer. Hour after hour, day after day, I leaned on the headboard of her metal bed and asked that my beloved daughter should be spared. I felt guilty asking for my own affairs without having the same intensity of feeling toward other children in the ward. When Ray came in, I used to go to the hospital chapel or sit outside where the world was carrying on, quite oblivious to the desperate drama being acted out in a tiny hospital side ward. Everyday life seemed surreal. Nobody on earth knew the intensity of feeling being played out inside my head – and why should they? To say I was desperate and despairing was an understatement. All I could do was stay externally calm and as gentle and cheerful as I could be for my sick child and the rest of my family. So I washed and rewashed her favourite toy, a squirrel by the name of Nuts, because she continued to vomit, even though she was in a coma. Only twice did I see the other children during those terrible weeks. Ray cared for them and we didn't want them to see Jackie as she was. One day, Ray and I spoke about Jackie's possible quality of life should she recover. The side effects of this disease were deafness, limb loss and brain damage. I confessed to Ray that I wasn't sure I could cope with this and care for the other members of the family as well. We also talked about her possible death. Never have I felt such emptiness, anguish, loneliness and absolute despair before or since.

Then, one evening, I was leaning on her bed head half asleep when suddenly, out of nowhere, I distinctly heard Pa's voice say: "She will be alright now, gal!" I jumped and looked around, thinking he must have come to visit. But there was no one there. I thought I was finally losing it. 'Gal' is something Londoners call others. It is an affectionate term and my father-in-law often used to say it to me. When Ray came in, I told him what I'd experienced and we laughed for the first time in weeks.

Miracle of miracles, the coma broke next day! The doctors said it was too early to tell if there was any brain damage, but Jackie recognised us and could speak, smiling weakly before lapsing into a deep sleep. I was advised to go home, see the other children and get a really good night's sleep in my own bed. It seemed strange to be going home, but once I was there it felt wonderful to make a fuss of the other children. Afterwards, I had a light supper, a hot bath and fell into bed. At about three a.m., there was a violent and insistent banging on the front door which woke everyone with a start. Fearing the worst, I followed Ray downstairs and there were two police officers, one man and one woman, asking to come in. They told us to sit down as they had some bad news. Of course we thought Jackie had taken a sudden turn for the worse and had died. Looking white-faced, Ray got hold of the male policeman by his tie and practically swung him off his feet, saying: "Just tell us!"

It turned out they had been trying to get hold of us since late afternoon, but we were not at the hospital as expected and nor had we yet arrived home. Pa had suffered a sudden heart attack and, despite sustained efforts to revive him, he had sadly passed away. Was there a connection between Jackie's coma breaking and her return to life and his passing away? Was I the link between the two, having heard his voice at the time of his passing? The police left and Ray immediately got on the telephone, arranging to go to London the next day. We all understood that only he would go. The next morning, I watched him leave. He was to be away until after the funeral, staying on to support his mother while she adjusted. Then George would return.

With the help of a really good friend called Della who lived nearby, I coped with juggling school times, hospital visits and all the other logistics involved. Then came the day when I was allowed to bring Jackie home. It was still not clear about any possible brain damage, so I was advised to take her to all the places she had been before to see if she could remember. On the day after Jackie's return, Heather said: "That's not fair. She's staying home and I have to go to school!" My reply was: "Sometimes, life does not seem fair. But, right now, it's Jackie's turn to suffer and be the centre of attention. One day, it will be yours."

Ray returned, a saddened man, but he was pleased to see Jackie home and we started taking weekend outings to zoos and other places of interest. We had been very lucky. Jackie was okay. She had a little trouble with her vision, but could remember what she had done and where things were. In another few weeks, she returned to school and managed just fine. But my problems were far from over. Tony went to the local shop to buy some icing sugar and was gone a long time. Just as I was getting somewhat irritated, he returned and told me he had brought someone with him. There was nothing unusual about that, so I said fine and in walked a policeman! As well as the icing sugar, Tony had pinched a potato gun. It wasn't worth very much, but he'd been caught in the act. What really annoyed me was that, if he wanted the wretched thing so much, he had enough money on him to buy it. He said it was a dare from some schoolmates.

Social reports followed. Then, when Ray was away again in London, the summons to the police station arrived. My brother- in law, Brian, was an ex-policeman himself and volunteered to come with us. As a result of the reports, we were told they were not going to prosecute, but Tony would have to appear in front of a Police Inspector to explain himself. A few days later, he and I went to the appointment. He was made to stand in front of the desk while I was seated comfortably in an armchair in the corner of the office. The thing that struck me was the difference between the way in which the

Inspector spoke to the two of us. He was charming and considerate towards me, hard and unyielding towards Tony. I was convinced that Tony was contrite when we left. But, years later, I asked him if it had made any difference to him and he said: "Not really."

When Ray returned once more, we discovered that Tony was having trouble with bullies at school. Ray said to pick on the biggest bully and stand up to him. Even if you get bloodied, you will only have to do it once and they will leave you alone. I was horrified at this suggestion and felt very upset when Tony returned the following day with a bleeding face, but he was obviously pleased with himself. And Ray was right. He did not have anymore trouble after that. That evening, he went to Air Cadets and promptly fell off a bench, breaking his arm. So he looked like a wounded warrior for a while.

One day, an irate mother knocked on the door to say she had seen one of my children throw half a brick and it had hit one of hers. After listening to her for a while, I confronted all three children and asked them if it were true. Tony said they had done it, but the brick had hit no one. We gave apologies all around, but the lady was not to be placated. Then I put my foot in it by asking her if she wanted me to wash the clothes involved. She thought I was being sarcastic whereas I was being literal. I had thought Skem to be an improvement on the unfriendliness and isolation we'd experienced in Wales, but now I was not so sure. I also became aware that there were kids using drugs at Tony's school the day I found a syringe in his bedroom. I went ballistic! He told me he had found it and was using it as a water pistol. This turned out to be true and, in my anxiety, I felt I had violated his trust. This gentle lad who had been a friend as well as a son began to keep his distance from me. Saddened but busy, life went on.

Not long afterwards, we moved to a lovely four-bedroom house the other side of Skelmersdale, far away from the crowded upstairs maisonette. Things seemed to be taking a turn for the better at last. When mother-in-law Gill came to stay for the first time since losing Pa, we had a huge laugh about my fourth pregnancy. I had used every form of birth-control on the market and still ended up having the same number of children as she had prior to the introduction of family planning!

The months passed and the day came. Ray was away, so I changed the bed and did all the housework, not wanting to go to the hospital sooner than I had to. Eventually, I walked to the phone box and called an ambulance before driving across town and knocking on Della's door to ask her to mind the children until Ray got back.

As always, she was pleased to help. She had four children of her own and a very supportive husband and was always there for me. A lovely ambulance man with children of his own also said to me on the journey: "There you go, love. Drop your dignity at the door on the way in and pick it up again on the way out. You know the score!" If only they had both known what their care and concern meant to me! Much to my relief, the negative expectations I had carried since the difficult birth of Heather did not materialise. A few hours later, a lovely placid baby boy whom we called Drew was placed in my arms.

At the age of 34, I had four children. On arriving home, Jackie and Heather ran to meet us and were thrilled to see us. Respectively seven and four years older than their new baby brother, they were besotted with him and, as a result, Drew had three mums. Years later, he said I was by far the most lenient of the three! He was an easy-going baby and great fun to have around. A few weeks later, Ray broke the news that the Red Cross was transferring him to Milton Keynes and we would have to move yet again. He would go on ahead and prepare the house and I would stay and pack up the lovely house we were living in. I just resigned myself to the move. It never seemed to matter what I thought or wanted, so I ceased to get upset about it. Off he went, telling me by phone that the allocated house was open plan and he thought I would like it. Unfortunately, it was quite dirty and he was busy cleaning it during any spare time he had. A couple of weeks later, we joined him...and I sobbed! The house was okay, but nothing like we had left behind. There were two bedrooms upstairs under the eaves and one downstairs along with a large, open-plan living and kitchen area. We did have a small, enclosed garden at the back which was a bonus. We made it a home quite quickly and the children made more new friends. We were the oldest people in the area, Milton Keynes being an overspill town for London. So it was mostly young couples just setting up home, a few having just one child. The town was so new there were just a few saplings and little green space or fully-grown trees. Very quickly I became the agony aunt for the newly married relationship issues and the young mums.

Ray was busy with work. The nearest hospitals were Northampton General and Stoke Mandeville, both of them a good half-an-hour away up and down the motorway. All of us became involved with the Red Cross Centre where Ray was based. It was a Day Centre for the elderly as well as being a work and training office. Jackie and Heather were thrilled when they heard the Centre was to get a visit from HRH The Duchess of Kent. They, as Red Cross cadets, were to form a part of the Guard of Honour. It was a big event and the whole town turned out to witness it. All of us were fascinated at the security and the protocol involved, especially as a toilet had to be set aside for royal use and laid out in a very specific way!

Running to get to one of the rehearsals, Heather was chased and bitten on the leg by a stray dog. This required stitches and a tetanus injection, but she was by no means put off. She insisted on still going to the ceremony. The night before, I washed the girls' white uniform shirts, forgetting I'd left a red T-shirt in the machine. They all came out pink! I was up most of the night, bleaching them and washing them repeatedly. I managed to get them white again and nicely ironed when the big day came, but the family was not amused! The Duchess was a lesson in grace and charm, so it was a lovely day that we all remembered fondly.

At this time, there was an ambulance strike and the army's Green Goddesses were being used instead. On one occasion, Ray was driving one of these ancient military vehicles and I was with him, accompanying a patient as well as going for a hospital appointment myself. A speeding motorist cut the Goddess up and Ray was heard to say in a voice loud enough to amuse our patient: "If we pass you later on smashed up, mate, we're not stopping!" Dropping the patient off safely, I attended my appointment and was told I was very lacking in iron and so anaemic that something was definitely wrong. This came as no surprise as I had an almost permanent period since Drew was born. Ray's work kindly pulled a few strings and, just four days later, I found myself in the London Women's Hospital with a very nice, kind carer provided to look after the children while I was away. An exploratory operation was to be done. To my amusement, I learned the surgeon had the same surname as me. The day after the op, he came to see me and said:

"Mrs Fraser?" To which I replied:

"Yes, Mr Fraser?" Then he said:

"I am very sorry to inform you that we have had to remove the carry-cot, but we have left you the playpen!" At only 35, a full hysterectomy had been performed. Finding myself surrounded by much older women bemoaning their fate and their pain, I decided I was going to recover fast – and I did! Ten days later, I was allowed home, but told to take it very easy. The local GP called Doctor James came and arranged for a home help and I languished as much as I could on the sofa with a pillow over my tummy to deter the kids from wanting cuddles. I don't know if they were more pleased to see me or I was to see them.

Doctor James became a regular visitor and was quite strict with me. Being about our age, however, he also became a good friend to us all. We were also given a home help. She was very willing, but took ages to do anything and soon I was badgering the doctor to let her go. I wanted my family back! Not only did I manage the family and do all the ironing, I also started to redecorate the house – much to Doctor James's consternation. It seemed I had a new lease of life. The children were wonderful and helped with things I found difficult and we all laughed a lot as they started to learn to take their turn with household chores and cooking. Unfortunately, Ray and Tony, who was now fourteen, did not always get on very well. Tony challenged Ray about his frequent absences and his general lack of help. Apart from cooking the occasional meal, Ray was never at home. One day, the two of them had a big row and, being almost the same size as one another, the only thing I could think to do was to stand between them and tell them both to shut up. I was aware that Tony was hurt and Ray was annoyed, but I could not say any more to either of them. I did not want to divide loyalties or make the situation any worse than it already was.

Chapter 7 - Dover Beach

Ray began being rather remote and absent, but I knew he was busy and we had had a lot to cope with. A growing family is always a financial drain, so I was determined to help out. I started an evening slimming club which I named 'Trim a Shape'. It consisted of gentle exercise, dietary advice and discussions for which I charged a weekly fee. It was a huge success and I opened two more clubs in other parts of Milton Keynes. These also proved popular. Just two hours three times a week was a manageable amount of time and it helped out financially. I also sold Avon from the house and at the local clubs.

One Saturday evening when I got in, Jackie said she was not feeling great. So I put her to bed and read her a story, telling her to come and get me if she woke in the night not feeling well. About 2 a.m., she came into bed with us and, as a result, fell asleep again. I woke about 6 a.m. and I knew – I just knew – she had meningitis again. It was the smell. I could never forget it. Ray told me not to be silly, but I was convinced and waited until 7 a.m. to phone the doctor, knowing that at a weekend this might not be popular. He said he didn't think it was meningitis, but he would come over once up and dressed just to be sure. An endless hour-and-a-half later, he arrived. By this time, 20-month-old Drew also showed signs of being unwell. Tony and Heather seemed fine. On seeing Jackie and Drew, the doctor changed his mind and said yes, he did think it could be meningitis, but he suspected it could be of the viral variety. We would know the score within 48 hours.

Tony agreed to take charge of Heather and promised to keep in constant telephone contact with us just in case either of them began to show any symptoms. It was an awful feeling leaving them on their own, but Ray and I had no choice but to be where we were most needed. An ambulance was called. Jackie lay on a stretcher, holding Ray's hand. I walked beside it, carrying Drew. Both of them had vomited all over me, so I smelled wonderful but didn't care. At Northampton Hospital, we were treated promptly and with courtesy and soon found ourselves in the Children's Ward, awaiting tests. Poor Jackie was given another lumber puncture, lying curled up on her side with the doctor behind her and me in front of her, holding both her hands tightly and talking to her all the time. Dozy but still conscious, she tried to smile. It was decided that Drew was too young and too active for a similar test, so they hoped to diagnose both cases from Jackie's results. They did just that and it was proven to be viral meningitis. Jackie was admitted at once. Being so much younger, Drew would just not leave me, so it was decided I would stay while Ray returned home and then come back later. Jackie looked pale, grey and totally lethargic. Drew did not look much better. He was only comforted by lying across me with his arms around my neck. The doctors decided to use a conglomerate of antibiotics on a drip. As we had not used any drugs previously, they started to work. By late evening, things had improved a little. The staff decided to sedate Jackie and let her sleep, suggesting I should take Drew home but come back the minute anything changed. Ray duly collected us. Although I was exhausted, I found it impossible to sleep because I was too busy watching Drew's progress and worrying.

When I arrived back at the hospital the following morning, Drew looked so much better that some of the ward staff asked me what he was doing there! He had improved so much, they did not recognise him. Jackie was also feeling much better and, when the ward sister told me that the worst was over, I found it hard to believe. Both of them had suffered from viral meningitis, a serious illness with a life-or-death outcome. Yet both of them were home again within two days. However, in the coming weeks, various others symptoms appeared. Drew was not able to speak much, but having a super-telepathic family, he did not really need to. We were all able to anticipate his wants and meet them before he had to ask. Also, there seemed to be some kind of interruption in his brain. He would be walking or running when his legs would suddenly give way and he would collapse. Tony was wonderful on these occasions, keeping me informed of any incidents and often carrying him home. Jackie had some trouble with her vision, experiencing slippage on occasions that caused blurring or making her see triple. Regarding both their post-hospital symptoms, the medics said we should wait and see how things went.

It was very hard to stop worrying at this time. When you have sick children, it's all too easy to anticipate possible problems and become anxious about them, even though they don't exist. So Ray and I tried to be practical. Drew started speech therapy that was to continue for many years to come. Jackie learned to stay indoors the moment her sight troubled her and to feel her way around, using familiar objects in the house. With lots of loving help from the family, Drew and Jackie gradually managed to overcome their problems. Meanwhile, having been such a support, Tony got some time to go out and about with friends. One night, he phoned me to say he was at a party at a school friend's house and there were drugs there. He asked me what to do. I replied by asking him what he thought he should do. He decided to phone the police anonymously and then come home. He did this and I realised this lad was growing up. I was so proud of him.

Then came the great bombshell! Ray arrived home one day looking very sheepish and said he was leaving. He had been having an affair with his secretary – also married – and they were leaving together and going to the USA. He packed his things and, in spite of my pleading, left there and then. I felt numb – shocked, shattered and distraught. I loved this man and we had shared so much. Little did I know, but worse was to follow. Money was missing from the Red Cross funds. The husband of the other woman was connected to the Press and, within days, the story was front-page news in the local paper. Taking the children to school, I became the subject of dirty looks and whispered comments. Knowing I was being talked about felt just awful. I was also deeply worried that the children would become the victims of their classmates' hostility. It felt as if we were all under a microscope and this was most unfair because none of us had done any wrong. The following weeks were a blur of loneliness and misery, only helped by the older brother of a friend of Tom's called Jeremy. He and his family were recent South African immigrants who understood social isolation only too well. They were pleased to be able to do something for others for a change. Perhaps it made them feel less vulnerable.

I went to the children's schools and officially told them what had happened. They promised to watch out for any bullying as best they could. I kept phoning Ray and eventually he agreed to meet with me in Dover as he waited for his visa. We met on the beach. It could have been the setting for a romantic reunion, like a dramatic and moving scene from a film. In fact, it was quite the opposite. He was cold and distant with me, so the little hope I had quickly faded. He was relentless and determined about his life. He was leaving in two day's time and that was that.

"What about the children?" I asked him. "You'll manage," he replied. Crying inconsolably, I drove home feeling utterly hopeless and in a very dark place indeed. Jeremy, who had minded the children, greeted me with warmth and real care. A few weeks later, he told me he had got a house in Ashford in Kent and was leaving Milton Keynes to search for work down there. He'd had no luck where he was and had relations who could help him find work in that area.

I sold Trim a Shape to a large weight concern company and this gave us a little money to live on for a while. I continued working for Avon and I also started selling for a catalogue as well, so we were able to muddle through for a while. Both jobs were flexible and allowed me to pop home from time to time to check on the children. One day, on rounding the corner at the end of the street, there was Tony riding a friend's motor bike without a crash helmet. Did he look surprised to see me! These unexpected visits proved to be a good deterrent and kept the children in line without being too heavy about it. Next came a call from the Red Cross asking if the head honcho called Claude could visit me. He came and was so very kind. He told me what had been going on and said that none of it was in any way my fault. Although they did not have to, the Red Cross intended to pay me Ray's last month's salary for which I was profoundly grateful. Claude also informed me that as the house was tied to Ray's job, so we would have to move out, but they would give me three months' grace. I felt sorry for the man. He was obviously very uncomfortable having to do what he had to do. At the same time, I couldn't do anything other than accept all his kindness as we were desperate. I loved my family so much and was terrified at the possibility of their having to be taken into care. Having been through that experience myself, I was determined it wasn't going to happen to them and would fight so that we'd all be able to stay together.

During all the recent visits to the hospital, it had become very apparent that it would be really helpful to know the health record of my genetic family. So I applied to get my natural birth certificate, my adoption certificate having served to date. A summons arrived for me to attend an interview in Preston, Lancashire. I was in two minds whether to go or not due to time and the money involved, but I did. It proved to be a daunting experience. Two men and one woman were sitting behind a desk at one end of a long hall, looking very imposing.

There was a chair for me halfway down the room. They questioned me as to why I wanted my natural birth certificate and I explained about the children. Then they asked me what being adopted had been like and I told them.

"Have you ever considered that your guardian might be your natural mother?" asked one of the stern-faced men. "She could have arranged the adoption because she did not want to admit to having a child out of wedlock."

"Yes, this had occurred to me," I replied. "But I don't think it's the case." "Why do you say that?" demanded the woman. "I just know," I answered.

Seeing their bewildered expressions, I hurriedly went on to explain that Betty had so obviously been unprepared for having children in the house and there was the fact that Jane had been adopted with me as well. Then the other man told me they would have to check that I was rational and that I would not run amok once given the information. I felt like saying I was sure I would not run amok, but I wasn't at all sure I was rational. But I just said nothing. I could not wait to get away! They gave me a piece of paper to present to Somerset House in London which would enable me to get my original birth certificate when required. Some weeks later, when I had the money, I did go to Somerset House where a kindly clerk helped me find the original birth certificate with my mother's name on it. As I had been born out of wedlock, my father's name was not there. So I did belong to someone after all! Why had I been given away? Now I would never know. Feeling sad and a little bitter, I wondered if I would be capable of facing the future. But as I did not know what else would be in store, I felt resigned to my fate. So much had happened, I felt exhausted at all levels of my being. So I just decided to concentrate on the next step.

Without Ray there, the children were all holding their own very well. They were my main concern during these difficult times. With the help of the speech therapist, Drew's talking improved. He was still stuttering and mumbling a lot, but he was really trying and that was what mattered. Jackie's vision also seemed a little more stable. But I was feeling worn down, exhausted and emotionally drained. Being a single parent again, this time with four children instead of one, I felt impotent and powerless, but I was absolutely determined to hold it together for the sake of the children. The three months grace kindly given to us by the Red Cross was rapidly running out. We would have to move soon. But where?

Jeremy kept phoning me up and calling round to see me. One day, he said to me: "Look, Judy. I have this four-bedroom house with only me in it. Come to Ashford away from all the gossip and start again. You can apply for housing in your own right if you like and there are plenty of jobs around here."

Not knowing what else to do, I agreed. I did not like Ashford from the moment we arrived. And it wasn't true that Jeremy was the only inhabitant of the house. His mother and father and his younger sister were all staying there, awaiting completion of their new house. We had no alternative but to muck in and manage. It felt sleazy and poor, but then beggars cannot be choosers.

Tony had just finished senior school and decided to go into the Services to get a degree. I couldn't afford university for him, so I'm sure he went into the Armed Forces because he was desperate to get away from home and have a life of his own. I did not blame him at all. Much to my surprise, he chose the Navy rather than the Air Force. He was accepted immediately and moved from Milton Keynes with us while awaiting entry. The deal for which he had signed up consisted of four years of study at university followed by three years paying back the investment. After that, he would be given the choice of staying in the Navy or being released. Meanwhile, he went to work in a local factory. The girls were enrolled in a nearby school which they tolerated. Drew went to playschool and I got a job at the local hospital, working in the operating theatre at night. It was an exhausting schedule and sleep for me was in short supply, but I managed.

Jeremy could not get enough of my company. He pursued me relentlessly. He was clearly the master and, all too easily, I fell into a subservient role. About a month after our arrival in Ashford, I was so exhausted, emotionally and physically, that I let him bully me into marrying him. It was a Registry Office ceremony attended by Jeremy's mother, father and sister – all of whom had applied similar pressure on me in their own way. They said it would be good for the children but, with the benefit of hindsight, I can see now they thought I would be a stabilising influence on Jeremy and they would be off the hook. I had no idea they were on a hook at the time...and it would be my turn next! Once married, Jeremy became even more possessive and stifling. Realising I needed a break, I decided to go down to Devon and see Betty. She still had some household goods in storage and, knowing she would never live on her own again, she wanted rid of them. So, one Bank Holiday weekend, I made a dash for it with Jackie, Heather and

Drew. We saw Betty for a brief while, but she was more interested in getting her valuable items of furniture out of storage and into local auction, just telling me to take what was left over. I also arranged for the local bank to transfer the funds from the auction into Betty's account. Then we left with a loaded van to get back in time for work and school. Jeremy was delighted at seeing his house being decked out with much nicer furniture than previously and could not have been more helpful with the unloading.

Apart from my children, the only bright spot for me was work. I loved the theatre team and all that I learned there. We had a strict theatre sister always known by the staff as 'Vadonk' (a parody of her real name Sister Van Donk) who would stand no nonsense. She was always on everyone's case regarding timing, uniform, cleanliness, overlong tea-breaks and other things. I made friends with a male nurse called Frederick who was nicknamed 'Porridge' on account of his obsession with porridge being good for you. Coming from Scotland, he had it for breakfast every single day, working or not. He was tubby, very kind and full of laughter. We had to wear rubber boots or clogs. Most of us chose the clogs, including Porridge who took the binding off and made vertical cuts in the sides so it was easier for him to get his fleshy feet into them. This was against regulations and he soon found himself going head-to-head with Vadonk.

"Frederick, why exactly are you wearing those shoes?" she asked in a disapproving tone. "Because they are regulation, Miss Van Donk," replied Porridge.

"Not in that state, they're not!" retorted Vadonk with considerable irritation. "They won't go on my feet without being fringed," explained Porridge. Vadonk was now very angry.

"Then your feet should lose weight," she said with absolute seriousness. "I find that rather insulting," sniffed Porridge. "They are against regulations and not antiseptic!" snapped Vadonk.

"The clogs or my feet?" asked Porridge. By now, Vadonk was almost beside herself with rage.

"You have not heard the end of this by any means," she roared. "I will be getting back to you!" "And I will be waiting and looking forward to that," answered Porridge with obvious amusement and great courtesy. None of us had ever been brave enough to call Vadonk's bluff like that before and, as a result, the conversation was a prominent subject in the staff room for weeks to come.

I also made friends with an anaesthetist called Dr Toms after showing interest in different states of consciousness. I told him about the children's illnesses and he tried to help me understand the different levels experienced via anaesthetic. He went on to explain what states of relaxation could be achieved via medicines and by natural methods such as yoga. I was hooked and never ceased to learn from Dr Toms whose knowledge always impressed me greatly.

Knowing I had a family, I was always asked to look after any post-operative children in the recovery room. With eight operating theatres on the go, we were always busy, even at night. Once, a disturbed post-op boy lashed out and unwittingly knocked my front teeth out. I was given five working days leave as a result to get my teeth fixed and recover from the trauma. It felt strange to be at home during the week. The house was looking nice with all Betty's furniture in it, but somehow it still did nothing for me. This wasn't helped by a minor disaster that occurred during this time. I was playing a game with the younger children when Tony came rushing in, shouting: "There's a fire upstairs!"

I went up to see and came rushing back down again, yelling: "He's right! Call 999!" The fire engines were there quickly. Tony, Jeremy and I had taken one child each and were standing outside, waiting for them to arrive. We watched, fascinated, as the firemen rushed through the kitchen with their hoses. The fire was soon out. Then the inspectors turned up to find the cause of the fire and decided a spark from somewhere had ignited a dressing gown and then the armchair it was thrown across. The smoke-damaged bedroom was very smelly, so we closed the door and all endured an uncomfortable and uneasy night downstairs. Luckily, no one was hurt and the damage was minor. I was just glad it was only us in the house and the room had been empty. Jeremy's parents and his younger sister had moved on, having been allocated a house.

Men kept calling, looking for Jeremy, and then the police. On the occasions I was in the house, I thought this was odd, but I was so absorbed in trying to survive that I took little notice. I was also inclined to take my husband at face value. Deep down, I felt imprisoned by this man, but unable to escape. One day, a policeman I knew from the hospital asked me what a nice girl like me was doing with a man like him. Suddenly, warning bells began clanging in my head! Thinking about it, I was an emotional prisoner and I wasn't really being treated well at all. Then I began to worry about the children. How were they being treated behind my back? I realised we had to escape and get out.

I knew I would have to do this with great caution and considerable planning. We were all a little frightened of Jeremy, having seen the extent of his temper on occasions. In fear and trepidation, I discussed the problem with Ali Simms, my boss at work. I was gratified to receive such an empathetic and sympathetic response from her. She told me of a woman who ran an outfit called Singlehanded. A few days later, I phoned and spoke to a warm, caring lady called Anne.

Anne had five children and had known hardship herself. Obviously identifying with my predicament, she was lovingly assertive and shocked me by saying I would have to move into a Women's Refuge so as to protect myself and the children. Hopefully, this would not be for long. She would meet me at a car park if I drove to Haywards Heath in Sussex and escort me to the premises. The people at the Refuge would know we were coming, but she would not divulge the address to me until we'd arrived to safeguard everyone concerned. It seemed all very clandestine and surreal, as if I were taking part in a cloak-and-dagger drama. It was only seven weeks until Christmas and Jeremy started watching us like a hawk. He sensed something was going on, so we all had to try and act as normal as possible. The day came. I piled a few items into the car and collected the children. Then off we went, leaving Christmas cards we had received just where they were to make everything look as usual and buy as much time as possible. Would our old banger make the 40-50 miles to our destination? We desperately hoped so! Stopping only for petrol and a well-deserved ice-lolly for the three children (Tony was now in the Navy), we duly arrived to be met by Anne and taken on to the Refuge close by.

There were five other families resident in the home. Some were obviously very damaged and kept themselves to themselves. Others were coping with sickness and a couple were just down on their luck. We were allocated a large room, but all the other facilities were shared. The staff were superb. On the first morning, I was interviewed by Gloria, the Refuge Manager, and asked to state our exact circumstances before being advised on State benefits, schools and so on. It felt very strange being at the Refuge. I was used to being in control, not being told what to do and how to live my life. Yet, oddly enough, it turned out to be one of the best Christmases ever. The children were relaxed and we spent a lot of time walking and playing in the park. Touchingly, they all bought me a small gift with their hard-earned pocket money. One was a dictionary from a supermarket which I have in my desk to this day.

Then Gloria discovered that Jeremy had found out where we were and had been snooping around. She had interviewed him outside and sent him packing. As a result, a Restraining Order was obtained from the courts. Clearly, Jeremy was fearful of any more contact with the law and so, months later, a divorce was granted with minimum fuss and we never had any contact with him again.

After Christmas, things began to pick up a little. Anne asked me if I'd be willing to give her a hand with Singlehanded. As my own experience had proved, her organisation was a lifeline for those who for one reason or another were coping with being a one-parent family. Not only did I find a purpose for myself in being able to support and encourage others, I also appeared to be really helpful to the clients and they started asking for me personally. Although I was not being paid for my services, I felt I was making a difference and this did me a lot of good. I also went to see St Joseph's, the local primary school. I was worried because St Joseph's was Catholic and we weren't, but the teachers were very helpful. They said they would welcome all the children when the term started and promised to keep an eye on them to make sure they settled in happily. Then I had to approach the DSS. Never having 'signed on' or been on benefits before, I had no choice now but to apply. I vowed it would be for the shortest time possible. Gloria also said that I was the type whom she expected would move on quickly which I thought was an encouraging thing to say. One day, when working for Anne, I met a woman called Aisha. She was very New Age and somewhat eccentric, but extremely kind none the less. She told me of a small row of five farm cottages all housing single parents who looked out for one another.

I decided nothing ventured, nothing gained and went with her to see the cottages. They were all fully occupied except for one which housed a young gay man. He wanted to house-share to save expense and so did I. It was a perfect match! The cottage was a pretty place with three bedrooms and was infinitely better than where we were. So we moved in and it proved a happy eighteen months for all of us before the farmer who owned the cottages sold the lot. At weekends, we borrowed bicycles from the other families and cycled for miles around the local lanes. We all began to look healthy again and the camaraderie we shared was lovely. If I was held up at work, I knew the others would mind the children – and vice versa. Tony came home on leave, bringing three friends with him. They slept end-to-end on the sitting room floor. They were good-natured lads who made a huge fuss of the younger children. It was a time of laughter and affection all round.

On another occasion, Jackie was asked if she would like to ride a horse and needless to say said yes. I was apprehensive as she still occasionally had trouble with her vision and, of course, something went wrong. Instead of walking gently up the lane, the horse was startled by a rabbit and bolted. My heart in my mouth, I bundled Heather and Drew into the car and followed, only to find the runaways a couple of miles up the lane. Jackie had a huge grin on her face and was not frightened at all while the horse was grazing peacefully on the grass.

Upon my return, I got a lecture from the other parents about being overprotective. Clearly, it was time for me to catch up. I needed to respond to where we were now and not to be stuck in the past.

One day, I was summoned to St. Joseph's. Drew had got into trouble. We were all vegetarian at the time because we couldn't afford meat. The school knew and adjusted the free school lunches accordingly. The prefect supervising the meal did not know this and kept on and on at Drew to eat up the meat on his plate. Drew was still having great difficulty in speaking and was doing well to even be in mainstream schooling. He tried to stutter some words of explanation, but was not given the chance. Eventually, in his frustration, he had punched this much bigger boy in the eye. When I arrived, the two boys were sitting side by side on small kindergarten chairs at a table with the Deputy Head in front of them. Despite his name – Mr Coward – this talented teacher dealt with the problem very skillfully. In front of both sets of parents, he told Drew he had been courageous to stand up for himself, but there was another way to deal with being bullied. He told the prefect that his behaviour was not acceptable and he had got a well-deserved punch as a result. He asked the parents if they wanted anything else done about the situation. We all said no and were sent home for the remainder of the day, normal service being resumed the following morning.

During the school holidays, my children teamed up with Anne's five children and had a wonderful time playing in the large garden while Anne and I continued to work. When we met parents in need, Anne would work in a room on one side of the house and I would occupy a room on the other. One day, much to our amusement, we were both interviewing new clients when a succession of nude children streaked past the windows. Neither of us was able to interrupt what we were doing to find out what had prompted this action. We found out later that they were pretending to be skinny-dipping, having found out from a book that it was something a bit naughty and wanting to see our reaction. We just told them you needed water and not grass and left it at that!

At the beginning of the following term, Jackie had to move from St Joseph's to St Paul's, its sister secondary school further down the road. Very tearfully, she and I walked there on the first morning having dropped the other two off first. She did not want to go to this daunting new school and my heart went out to this poor child who'd experienced so much already in her young life. Trying to be empathetic, the only thing I could think to tell her was that by law she had to attend and she could either make it a positive or a negative experience. Whether she took notice or not of what I said, she did come out smiling at the end of the day.

When the farmer gave us all notice and told us to move out, I began to question if we were always going be victims of the actions of others. But there was no time to feel sorry for myself. I had to set about finding alternative accommodation. All I could find in the school catchment area was a huge house which was let off into rooms by a man called Shawn. I took one and we moved in, but it was with a sense of trepidation and I couldn't work out why. I found out soon enough. The house was beautiful and the enormous garden a work of art, but Shawn was a severe epileptic and somewhat moody as a result. I was never quite sure how to take him. Sometimes, he was confused and demanding. On other occasions, he was charming and seemed to love the lively atmosphere of a growing family. My problem was how to keep the balance and be inclusive of all. Often feeling overstretched and anxious, I loved it when Tony and his friends came on leave again. Their banter was fun and they were generous with time for the younger ones, building them a wonderful tree-house in the garden. They also contributed towards their keep, knowing I could not afford to feed them all. Even so, there was such a lot of extra work cooking mountains of food which had to be shopped for, prepared and cleared up.

Before long, I found myself working at two jobs. In addition to Singlehanded, I became PA to a young man called Peter who had worked for Olivetti Business Machines and had recently left to start his own distributorship. He wanted a personal assistant because he was married and had three young children, one of whom was profoundly handicapped. This meant he often had family commitments that had to be attended to. He decided, with my background, I was just the person he was looking for. He was very understanding and sympathetic about my circumstances and I was the same with him. Having up-fronted my entire situation to him (including the fact that I was technophobic) we started a happy association that was to last. He said my job was to teach people to overcome their fear of having a go on the machines rather than to be competent at working all of them myself. He would just get me up to a basic minimum and the technicians would do the rest. Phew! With his trust in me and a belief I would be able to understand the machines, I slowly gained the confidence to become good enough, although I often had to admit when I had reached my limits.

By now, Shawn was becoming impossible to live with and I found out that he did not own the house at all. It was a part of an estate and he was just the tenant. I went to see the Estate Manager who turned out to be very understanding and told me he had a farm cottage becoming available shortly and we could have that. I'd kept my vow and was now off benefits, but I was on a low income which meant the children still got free school meals. We moved to the cottage and we all loved it. Two-up and two-down, it was our little haven. The children were all upstairs; I had one room downstairs. The living room was small but cosy. Then there was a bathroom and kitchen with a big back garden. The children were growing and flourishing and had many friends who were constant callers at the house. I used to go out and dig in the garden from time to time. Nobody liked this chore except me. I found it gave me some peace and quiet which I badly needed.

Jackie told me one day that she was made to feel ashamed at school for having free school meals. Those who did were ostracised by the other children. She said she did not want to have lunch any more. I said that was fine – or there was another way she could go. She was on the School Council. So I suggested that she could work to get the system changed. Bravely, this was the route she chose to follow and the entire system was changed as a result of her efforts. I almost burst with pride at her achievement – indeed, at all of my children. Life had been very hard for them and they had all handled it so well. On fine days, they walked the mile to school and back, the girls making sure Drew was delivered and fetched. There was never any quibble or resentment at having to do this or many other chores. One morning, there was a road accident just down the road from our cottage. The first I knew about it was Jackie and Heather rushing to get blankets. On going back with them, I saw it was a severe accident and other motorists were helping the best they could until the ambulance and police arrived. Although badly shaken, all three children insisted on going on to school. They were a credit to themselves.

After a while at the new cottage, strange things began to occur. The telephone used to ring, but there was no one there. This happened day and night for months on end. The telephone company agreed to censor our calls, but it did not stop these unwanted ones. The police said there was nothing they could do. My nerves were fraying at the edges and I was tired because the phone was situated in my bedroom. I found out that this kind of psychic phenomenon occurs quite often where children are going through puberty. It lasted for a year, then stopped as suddenly as it had started. I also developed backache which grew worse and worse until I was forced to consult our local GP, Dr Fulford, with whom I had developed a friendship as he attended Shawn so often. Arriving in his surgery and announcing that I was suffering from a persecution complex, he laughed and asked if I wanted to see a psychiatrist. To our mutual surprise, I said: "Yes, please! I want to make sure I'm sane!" He arranged it and I had three long sessions with a psychiatrist called Dr Bridewell. Afterwards, he assured me I was quite sane, but understandably stressed.

In due course, Dr Bridewell reported back to Dr Fulford. Amused by my antics, Dr Fulford asked us all to supper. He had one child and, from then on, our families saw a great deal of each other. One day, his wife Bridget asked me if I would go with her to listen to a talk being given by a chiropractor called Peter Goldman quite near us. Her husband would do the child-minding at my house. "Why not?" I thought to myself. My back hurt enough and the chiropractor might be able to give me a few pointers on how to ease the pain. After a half-hour drive, we arrived at this beautiful house which was packed with people all vying for a seat. Sitting near the back of the room, I listened spellbound. Not only did Peter Goldman, chiropractor, talk about bad backs, he also talked of the spirit which animated the body that had to be kept fuelled. This could be supported by meditation practice and also by conscious awareness of the beauty nature provides so abundantly. No one wanted this talk to finish, least of all me. To my surprise, on leaving, Peter Goldman shook my hand and told me to make an appointment to see him about my back. How did he know?

Was my body language so obvious? I never found out. I was content that Bridget had his address and phone number.

Weeks later, I decided to visit Peter Goldman. So I saved up the fee and made an appointment. His consulting room was a front room in his house. As I walked in, I was greeted by his wife Suzie and their three children. The whole atmosphere of the place was one of light and love. It seemed to glow, as did the people. The children were so normal and happy-go-lucky. It was a lovely, relaxed home. Peter was very professional and reassuring as he examined my back. He seemed in no hurry, talking as he prodded and probed. He told me my back would feel sore and I would need to come back in a week.

"Can you afford it?" he asked. "No, I can't," I answered, truthfully. He looked deep into my eyes and said he would have to charge for this appointment, but there would be no charge for the next. That was a follow-up procedure and was as much for his benefit as my own. He said he wanted to consult with some colleagues and then to see me again. I thanked him, thinking at the time it was all a little odd when he explained that the next session would take longer than the first. Then I left for home. The next day, my back was stiff and sore, but definitely felt better. That was a great relief.

The days passed and it was time for my second appointment. I was about to get far more than I had expected! Peter was pleased to hear his back treatment had been successful and said he'd spoken to various colleagues and they all wanted to meet me. "It's out of the question!" I said, emphatically. "I'm already finding it hard to cope with work, my involvement with Singlehanded and the family. Not to mention money. That is always an issue and everything I earn is spent already..." "Whoa, whoa," he soothed, gently and kindly. "It's both necessary and essential for the well-being of us all that you meet my colleagues. As for money, there would be no charge for the visit and any other expenses would be covered by this..." With that, he slipped two hundred pounds into my jacket pocket! Never having experienced such kindness, care and spontaneous generosity before, I was quite overcome. I didn't know how to respond, so I burst into tears! Sobbing, I agreed to meet his colleagues at their healing college.

I went a few weeks later, one Saturday when Tony was home on leave again and could look after the children. Peter was there already. The College Principal, a woman called Cicely, showed me around. First we looked at a beautiful lecture hall in the shape of a pyramid. She told me how it had been built and the difficulties they'd experienced getting the roof just right. Tiered seating and a central platform made for superb acoustics. Then there was a small chapel called the Galilee made from a shed that monks of old had used when they came in from the fields for their lunch. The atmosphere of this place just blew me away. It had abiding peace and an 'otherness' that was tangible. Cicely was watching me closely when I said how beautiful it was and how utterly familiar it felt. There were two staff cottages next to the Galilee and then the office and accommodation block for students. This had a large covered conservatory the length of the building with eight student rooms on the first floor.

White Lodge, as the place was usually known, was a college for spiritual psycho-therapeutics or soul sickness. This was something Peter had reported and I had already experienced. As a result of this soul sickness, people often developed gifts that were inherent in their personalities. They had to be taught how to use them, otherwise they could harm themselves and others by becoming insular, neurotic or even psychotic. And the gifts that were manifesting themselves were not a destination in themselves but a step on the journey. I was fascinated and could have listened to these 'normal' practical people for hours. Then it was coffee time. Cicely and I were joined by Cicely's husband, Jack, along with an old friend and colleague called Joyce who had known the founder of the college, the late Ronald Beesley. Ron, or RPB as he'd been affectionately known by all, had founded the college in Kensington in London during the war to aid those who were stressed to come to terms with changes in their lives. Later, when demand had become too great, he had moved to this location in Kent.

The college offered seven courses at one a year. It used to be one course every two years, the idea being that the long gaps in between gave people the time to integrate what they learned into their lives up to that point. As long as people were able to do this and respond with grace, it was now deemed possible to speed this up to one a year. I was told this by Peter before he went off to join the other directors to talk about an important issue that had just come up. I was left to my own devices and drifted off into the gardens. I wanted to visit the Galilee again anyway. An hour later, Peter and Cicely came to find me. They said the meeting had been all about me and, unanimously, they wanted to offer me a full scholarship to take all seven courses. They considered me to be an investment to both spirituality and to life. I laughed when I heard this and commented, with my chequered history, they had a very biased view.

"Not so!" insisted Cicely. "Often people with difficult backgrounds have the most talent as they are forced to have a great deal of experience very quickly as life tests their mettle." I felt humbled and deeply grateful for their amazingly generous offer, but there were major obstacles in the way of my taking it up. "I just don't see how it's going to be possible to find the time with the commitments I already have," I protested. They were not to be dissuaded and took no arguments from me. "Baby-sitters can be arranged and work done from home," explained Peter. "We will personally mentor you. A lot of the practical details are already in place..." On and on he went until I gave in. "Yes, okay!" I said. "I will give it a try!" Hopefully, this was not too ungracious. I just didn't know how I was going to cope with the increased workload. I did not want to have even less time than I did already for the children.

The expression about taking to something 'like a duck to water' comes to mind. I had found my intellectual and spiritual home! Long into the night, I would be studying and working. At this time, Anne sold her house and moved away from the area. Sorry as I was to see them go, I could no longer work for Singlehanded and that meant I had more time. My first thesis was written in 1983 and, to my surprise and elation, I gained 99 out of 100! As a result of this, I was told to continue studying at my own pace, but with mentorship and supervision. The aim was to give me a strong foundation in all aspects of metaphysics and spirituality and then to specialise in any aspect of interest. Some years later, all seven theses were completed and I gained an overall average of 98%. The children were thrilled for me and didn't mind the time I'd spent studying because I was so much happier. All of us were thriving, comparatively speaking.

One day, I was called to the college for a meeting. I was given my qualification certificate, but that was not the end of it. I was also offered a full-time job at the college, along with living accommodation in one of the staff cottages. It didn't take me long to say "yes, please!" Jackie had passed all her GCSEs very well and was about to go on to Sixth Form College. Heather was in her last two years at school and Drew would shortly be moving from the Infants into mainstream primary school. So it seemed as good a time as any for a change. All of the family agreed it would be a good move and I would be doing something I loved. When I handed my notice into the business system job, it was with regret on both sides. Peter had been a wonderful boss and kindly said I had helped his family to cope with their difficulties to a large degree. If ever I wanted my job back, I only had to call him up.

So off we went. The children loved the freedom and the lively atmosphere of the college and I loved the work. It was a happy and expansive time for us all and I found it easy to combine work, school and home. Jackie loved the Sixth Form College she went to and made some friends there with whom she is still friends to this day, 25 years on. Heather met and became friends with another girl called Jo and they were inseparable. As the youngest member of the family, Drew got lots of attention from one and all. It must have been a relief for him to find some male company and many lads were found kicking a football around with him in the times to come. After seven years, Tony decided to leave the Navy and attend university again. He wanted to get another degree, this time in psychology. As a mature student, he got a good grant and went to Keele in Staffordshire. As a result of this, we did not see so much of him, but we kept in touch by phone.

On October 16th 1987, a hurricane swept across the South of England and Kent was one of the places worst hit. This was soon after we had moved to White Lodge. The whole of the surrounding area was devastated by the winds. Trees came down, buildings were badly damaged, electricity was cut off. It was chaos! I was scheduled to go to see a publisher, but I couldn't even get out of the college driveway. For a week, we walked the two miles to the local shop, climbing over fallen trees. There was extensive damage at the college, but until the roads were cleared nothing could be done. An eerie silence descended and we felt like pioneers surviving on minimum provisions with no means for cooking or washing. The children loved it, whereas the adults found it somewhat trying! Over the following weeks, order gradually began to emerge out of the chaos and confusion. Roads reopened and builders quoted on the repairs. Drew developed a bad dose of measles at this time, but spent his time drawing cartoons and listening to rap music which he tried to emulate with some success.

Jackie was thriving and Heather and Jo were like twins. They were never apart, either at Jo's house or ours. One night, Heather and Jo went to a party at a school friend's house. Just as I was expecting them to come home, I got the call that every parent dreads! It was the police telling me there had been a bad road traffic accident and the girls were being taken to the local hospital. My neighbour minded Drew as I dashed to the hospital where I was taken straight to Heather. She started crying directly after she saw me, telling me Jo was bad. She did not look too good herself. Recalling what I'd said to her years ago when Jackie was suffering, she asked me if it was her turn now. "Too right," I replied.

She was in a neck collar and had hurt her back. 24 hours later, after extensive examination, I was told to take her home, but keep a close eye on her. Jo was not so fortunate. She had broken her back. Another girl was also kept in and yet another had died. It turned out the car was overloaded and the driver, who'd had a drink, had been messing about and had lost control. He was an older boy who was later charged with dangerous driving. He was fined and his licence was withdrawn for two years.

Desperate to be at Jo's bedside, Heather badgered me to take her back to the hospital. Jo's mum, who was a District Nurse, was desperately trying to get hold of her ex-husband, Jo's father, who was on holiday in the Greek Islands. The police were also trying to track him down. An urgent decision had to be made about whether or not to turn off Jo's life support system. Eventually, in consultation with the doctors, it was decided the machine was to be turned off. Jo's mum could not face this unbearable ordeal and asked me to sit with Jo while she and Sam waited in an ante-room. I considered it an honour and a privilege. I talked to Jo and told her what was about to happen. Telepathically, she told me it was what she wanted and she was ready to go. Feeling the presence of absolute peace and calm, warmth and care, I was certain she had been met by and was now being cared for by beings who had gone before. It was an amazing time and one never to be forgotten. Their local priest arrived and I went to join the others. Jo's organs were being donated and still her father did not know.

The following days were both sad and busy. Between sobs, Heather told me that Jo was in the invisible realms but their bond was life-long and she would be supervising work that Heather would eventually be doing here on the earth. I believed her. Jo's dad returned to the tragic news of his daughter's death and he and his ex-wife decided that Jo's life was to be celebrated as well as mourned. The funeral service attracted more than 200 people. Teachers, school friends, friends from the army cadets of which Jo was a keen and active member merged with relatives, neighbours and family friends. Julie Felix, a well-known folk singer from the 60s and an old friend of mine, had written a song for Jo which was played at the service. It included the line: "I'll meet you there where the sea meets the sky."

Julie had performed a concert at the college on the night that Jo's life support machine was turned off. A recording of the song was played again at the funeral service as a tribute. Both on the night of the concert and at this service, there was not a dry eye in the house. The song captured the imagination of everyone present. The children had learned it word for word and they sang it at the service with gusto. It was a never-to-be-forgotten memory and the first time I saw a smile on the faces of Jo's parents since the tragic accident.

Standing in the college kitchen after the service, I felt spent and empty. Peter found me there and made me a cup of tea. He was so loving. He assured me there was no more to be done and our job (not my job) was to get Heather over this huge hurdle to enable her to move on with her life. For two long years, Heather slept on the floor of the sitting room, the only place she could get comfortable. Peter worked on her neck and back until eventually the collar came off. She went back to school just to do her exams and did well but found concentrating on them almost impossible. Time does heal and life continued. Tom brought Roberta, his intended wife, home to meet us. Meanwhile Jackie, still at Sixth Form College, had won the Youth of Exceptional Promise Award that was to give her a summer holiday post of working at Chichester Festival Theatre. She was to be in a play starring Donald Sinden and get work experience both in front of house and behind the scenes. She had also won a place on a much sought-after degree course on Arts Administration at Leicester. Nice things were beginning to happen again at last!

What did I feel I had learned from all these experiences? I had learned that insecurity and bad things still happen, but when we experience a connection to our inner selves then the outer is more manageable. We can all learn to unite inner and outer reality in a connection described by mystics of all persuasions. We can keep a lightness and buoyancy and have a loving attitude, but only if it becomes an integral part of us. It has to be a real part of our daily lives and not a pretence or something we got out and dusted off just when we needed it. Yes, we lose it at times of stress, but if we know we lose it, then we can do what's necessary to get it back again. If we practise, we can find a way to contribute emotional energy to others rather than stealing energy from them. This is not possible if we try to take control of or manipulate others. We have to retain a sense of equality and freedom to be able to support others and, at the same time, to encourage them to stake their claim to it too. It's no good if we preach or 'get weird' because we just get mocked and ridiculed. As a living demonstration of our beliefs, we are far more convincing. To question, then dream; to meditate and pray, we receive guidance and then, as our intuition develops, we are led to answers from within our living experience. This is provided by the wisdom of other human beings or from our own life experiences. We can increase these happening by uplifting others who have lost hope. By enhancing the growth of others, all of us remain secure ourselves in spite of living through difficult circumstances.

Chapter 8 - A Rant At The Universe

Learning how to let go of old beliefs requires us to surrender some of the fabric that has made us who we are. That means we must find out who we are at regular intervals because, as ideas change, we are not who we once were. We also have to face some unpalatable truths about ourselves, usually presented to us by others. That takes courage. I knew the children had this, so maybe I would find some too.

Tony got married to Roberta. Jackie was staying with them and was to take a prominent part in supporting him. Heather, Drew and I went up early the day of the wedding. It was to be held in a pretty church in Mill Hill with the reception being held at a country house nearby. It was nice to see all of the children so pleased to see each other. Hopefully, this would be a happy social occasion. It had not occurred to me to think Tony would want me as a part of the line-up at the reception, but he came to find me. Both Roberta's mother and I got huge floral bouquets as a thank you. I was quite overwhelmed and somewhat suspicious, it has to be said. Having been kept at a distance ever since his graduation, I'd kept as low a profile as I was able. Although this hurt me deeply, I recognised that it was an essential part of his bid for freedom and individuality. Jackie was very keen to be close to them, especially as Tony and Roberta had been super-supportive of her while she was at university. Clearly, I was being cast in the role of the anti-Christ. Only with the amazing counsel and support of their local vicar, I managed to hold it together. Getting on well with the bride's parents helped me greatly. In fact, when Roberta's father died, the only acknowledgement that I had been excluded to such a level but now re-included and forgiven came with being invited to throw a handful of earth onto the coffin by my daughter-in- law. I asked myself if I had been neglectful or jealous or had done something terrible and irresponsible in the past or if I had been reading the situation correctly? Whatever had gone on now seemed concluded. Was it a done deal and could I overcome my pain? I hoped so.

By now, we had stopped living at White Lodge and moved back to Haywards Heath in Sussex. Heather was tired of school and asked if she could leave and get a job. I agreed to this. She tried several positions before being sent to help out at a large public house owned by Whitbread. She loved the work and the landlords were very warm and supportive of her. She went from being a damp squib to rising star within months! Meanwhile, Drew had transferred to St Paul's, the secondary school that both the girls had attended a few years ago. The only condition for his entry was that we had to live in the school's catchment area. So we rented a lovely, large rambling cottage on the outskirts of Haywards Heath where we were to live for years. We had a landlord from Heaven who could not do enough for us. If he came on a routine inspection and thought any of the equipment was looking old, the next day he would phone and say a new one was being delivered regardless of whether the old one was broken or not. So, with a new base and White Lodge within reasonable travelling distance for me, things had all settled down very nicely. And Drew was happy again at school, having been miserable in the one in the White Lodge catchment area.

One of Drew's friends, an older boy called Ed, came to lodge with us. Drew trained with him after school in athletics and martial arts, so they had shared interests and became great friends. Ed was a joy to have around and watched out for Drew when I was not there. It worked wonderfully well. Life was good and peaceful and there was plenty of room for us all, including the many friends who came to call or stayed overnight. Meanwhile, I was really keen on establishing an outreach programme for the college which meant working for other organisations and having their people work at the college in return. In my opinion, it could not be whole or holistic any other way. These two ways of working should be complementary, yet very few practised this. A few did, however, and I would be their guest on many occasions.

One winter's night, when Ed was away and there was a minder at the house looking after Drew, my ancient car broke down on the M3 motorway on my way home. I used one of the roadside telephones connected to the motorway police. They told me, as a woman travelling alone, they would send a breakdown truck within half an hour. While I was waiting, I made a very strong statement to the Universe. If those above wanted me to continue with this type of work, then I needed a car that was not stuck together with string and chewing gum! The breakdown man duly arrived and told me it was something to do with the fuel tank. He said he would have to drain all fuel off down to the bare minimum to get to another Service Station. It was now after midnight, so I phoned the sitter who very kindly said, under the circumstances, she would stay on, but it would have to be on double time. The mechanic got the car going again and led me to the nearest petrol station open at that time of night. Thank goodness he did! I would never have found it without him. I filled up and he waited to see me on my way. I never forgot his kindness. He just brushed off my effusive thanks and patted my arm, saying "safe, uneventful journey!"

A short while later, my rant at the Universe was answered in the most convincing manner. Someone I knew called Georgina, a lady I'd supported along with her two daughters when they'd had to face some tragic circumstances, telephoned and asked: "Do you still have that old tattered car you used to drive about in?" "Yes," I replied. "Why do you ask?" "Well, we've just come into some money," explained Georgina, "and would like to demonstrate our thanks to you for what you did for us when we were in need. We will trade your old car in against the new one we are buying and you can have the car we are driving now as a gift."

It was a Subaru, just four years old! I couldn't believe it! "That's a clear sign," I thought to myself. "I am supposed to keep working in the direction I am going! So be it!" To give the Subaru a trial, Drew and I took it on our next three-monthly 'death run', driving down to Devon to see Betty. The car was a joy! Subaru were rally cars, so went like the wind and we no longer had to keep worrying about whether we were going to break down.

Jackie and three of her friends called to admire the car and to spend a day with me en route to Prague where they were seeing in the New Year. Tony had started this custom when he was in the Navy, welcoming in the New Year from a different city in a different country each time. Now with a child, Seth, the baton had passed to Jackie. Seeing them off, I didn't expect to set eyes on them again until a week later. To my amazement, I saw them on the television the very next evening! A New Year programme was doing the rounds of European cities and there they all were, grinning and waving like mad. Nice to know they had arrived safely, then!

Ed now had a steady girlfriend called Kate who spent so much time at our house that Ed asked if I would mind if she moved in. It seemed like a good idea as I was now getting work invitations from abroad. I needed to take these up, but money was still a constant problem. In this way, it meant there would be an older couple available to look after the house and keep an eye on any children at home. I always hated leaving Drew, but he wasn't a baby any more and, as they say, needs must.

Chapter 9 - One Surprise Followed By Another

My years of study at White Lodge meant that there was a great deal happening inside my head. I was becoming aware that getting people to acknowledge their spiritual life was not enough. Too easily, they created a divorce within their lives between their spiritual self and their human self. This seemed to me to cause all sorts of chaos within families, separating them rather than uniting them. Having meditated and prayed for years, it seemed I was able to ask questions in prayer and when least expected – out in the garden or going for a walk – the answers came. I was told by my inner thoughts to leave the safety of the college and to set up a service by myself. This came as something of a shock. It pressed all my insecurity buttons and made me feel very fearful and inadequate. The fact that it was being done *through* me and not *by* me helped considerably. When I wondered who would take care of the family, my innermost self responded with a question: "What makes you think you are the best person to care for them?" This made me ask if I was deluded with my own grandeur these days. Was I so superior and self-important that I had assumed only I was the best thing for my children? If I wasn't, then was I not good enough? What should I do and how should I behave? I expected to care for my children and wanted to do this, but had I assumed too much? Was it too late now that they were all getting older and not in need of the constant attention I had been unable to give them? Was I being found to be wanting? So many questions and so few answers!

To leave the college seemed like the onset of madness. I had been offered the Headship of White Lodge, but had turned it down as a gesture of loyalty and gratitude to those who had supported and encouraged me. Now I was thinking of leaving the place altogether and striking out on my own. Did I have delusions of grandeur or was I being difficult and causing waves? Asking my friends and colleagues for their opinions did not help much, either, because their comments were all so diverse. My only answer was to turn within and be guided by my intuition. After all, what was there to lose?

I went to another organisation as a facilitator. That is a teacher who will not stand above those who seek his or her knowledge and guidance. I met some fellow facilitators who encouraged me to follow my inner dictums. Then two strange events also took place that furthered my resolve to take heed of spiritual forces. The first was an encounter with another intuitive called David Cousins at a residential gathering. We found we had been given accommodation next door to one another and were sleeping head-to-head either side of a wall. I experienced a terrible skin rash all over my body which lasted for weeks. Meanwhile, he developed a kidney problem. Being a Water sign myself and he a Fire sign, had we triggered something in each other by working all day and sleeping head to head at night? We became good friends and rang each other up every day to find out how we were getting on, speculating for hours as to possible meanings.

The second event was very sad. An old colleague of mine called Don Copeland, who had supported what I was trying to achieve in getting all spiritually minded organisations to work together, died during a course at which he was present. I took over the course and tried to shield his shocked family from the speculative gaze of those attending the course. This made me stronger in my resolve to put a mechanical structure in place so that our inner and outer experience could match and marry. Then something *really* strange happened that appeared to put a major obstacle in the way of my striking out on my own!

It happened at another course I was attending. The manager interrupted a session to say there was an urgent telephone call for me in the office. Thinking something must have happened at home, I went to the phone having made my apologies to the people on the course. Then I experienced one of the most bizarre calls I've ever had! "Hello, Mrs Fraser," said a posh voice. "My name is Christopher Lake from Thomson, Snell and Passmore. I regret to inform you that Mrs Audrey Barker has died and left you her two children, Bronwyn and Michael, in her will."

"Stop messing about, Tony," I ordered, thinking my eldest son was playing a joke on me. "This is neither the time nor the place, as you well know." This baffled poor Christopher Lake who kept insisting this was a genuine call and everything he was saying was true. But how could it be? I did not remember anyone called Audrey Barker and I needed two more children like I needed a hole in the head! Eventually, I had no alternative but to believe him. Calling another advisor in to continue the course, I left to try to find out what this was all about.

Once again, truth turned out to be stranger than fiction. It seemed that Audrey had attended a course I had given over four years ago on care for kids in trauma. As I now had a reputation as someone who worked to resolve abusive situations, she had decided to co-name me with her husband in her will as her children's guardians. She knew she was dying of cancer and suspected her husband of having an affair, so she had named me in the will in case his circumstances became too messy to safeguard the children's welfare. What she hadn't known was that her husband had an undiagnosed brain tumor and had died three days after her. Both of them had older children from previous marriages. She had a ballet-dancing daughter who was married to an effusive and opinionated Greek guy. The father also had three grown-up children who were respectively a doctor, a dentist and a lawyer. Were any of them prepared to take on their orphaned half-brother and sister? Of course they weren't! They just argued with each other, like a debate between the Arts and the Sciences, as to best courses of action.

As far as I could see, the two children concerned seemed to have been completely forgotten. I talked with my own family and we all agreed we had to offer them somewhere that was relatively normal to live. So Bronwyn, aged thirteen, and Michael, aged twelve, came to stay with us. Whether this was to be a permanent arrangement or not was still undecided. I met them for the first time at the funerals of their parents. After that, we continued to meet every day. The pair of them were shocked and traumatised, both by the sudden loss of both their parents and, even worse, the constant squabbling of their grown-up half-brothers and sisters. They needed no persuasion and asked point-blank if they could come to my house to get away from all the quarrelling. I was happy to oblige, but at the same time I felt deeply concerned for Drew, also twelve, and Heather, now sixteen, feeling this was too big an emotional ask after all the traumas they had already undergone. How wrong could I be! I felt put to shame by their generous and accommodating stance. Jackie, almost nineteen now, and Tony were also very supportive of these less fortunate souls and offered their help and expertise. Delighted as I was at their generosity of spirit, I remained very concerned at the logistics. Where would we all fit in? How would I organise my existing work around two more young teenagers who still needed supervision, not to mention branching out on my own. It seemed too complicated to work out, so I decided one step at a time was the only course of action.

Eventually, it was decided that Michael would continue at the school he attended in Tunbridge Wells, staying with one of his half-brother's family during the week returning to ours at weekends and for holidays. Bron, on the other hand, was to attend Warden Park, the largest secondary school in Haywards Heath, and live with us all the time. In the weeks to come, the headmaster of Warden Park and the social worker concerned with this case did so much above and beyond the call of duty that it was humbling. Michael and Drew got on well together. Bron, on the other hand, seemed to get on with no one – including herself! Often, she would not speak at all to anyone. At other times, she would have a go at the boys for no apparent reason. She would lock herself in her room and not come out and would never join in without creating a drama which was very difficult and unfair to others. Thinking it would be good to give the newcomers a break, I left Jackie and Heather with Ed and Kate and took them to the Isle of Wight for a week along with Drew and a good friend of his called Nigel. What a disaster! The rain pounded down, the accommodation was inadequate and damp and it cost an absolute fortune trying to keep them all amused. Meanwhile, I set about some business of my own. Knowing that my birth mother originated from the Isle of Wight, I placed an advert in the local newspaper, saying if anyone knew anything about Alice Hayles please contact the box number (I knew my mother's name from the birth certificate I'd obtained from Somerset House). It was just three lines and appeared in the personal column of the local paper on one occasion only. I had several reasons for wanting to find out anything I could. Obviously, I was deeply curious to know more about my real mother. I also needed to know about my family's health patterns and history. And, on a practical level, if I could somehow prove my father's Canadian identity, then it would be so much easier to obtain a permit to work in Canada. As that was where I was committed to going next, at least I could tell the authorities I'd done all I could!

By now, the decision regarding my working status had been taken. I had left White Lodge and branched out on my own as an independent spiritual advisor. I called my organisation 'Second Aid'. It was a service devoted to the alleviation of stress through meditation, knowledge and self-awareness. But, now being self-employed, my income was more irregular than it had been while I was in permanent employment. So I began working abroad to earn some much-needed cash. At first, these were just short stints in Europe which were easier to balance against the demands of my newly increased family. But my forthcoming trip to Canada put me in a quandary. It was for two weeks rather than a few days and I was torn between knowing more money was needed and the somewhat difficult situation I was leaving behind. However, assured by everyone concerned that they could cope, I set off on my first major working trip abroad.

While I was in Canada, I was taken to meet a Shaman from a Native American tribe called the Cree Nation located near Montreal. It was fascinating! He was wearing jeans and a vest and didn't look anything like how I'd imagined a Shaman to look. We sat on his verandah, drinking tea. Later, he took me inside his house to see his drum collection. One by one, he showed me the tools of his trade. Then he held my head in one hand and blew into my ears, after which he drummed. I was sure deafness would result! Mercifully, it didn't. Nor did the technique have the desired effect on me. It does have the power to transport you to other dimensions of awareness that are beyond words and very, very holy. Thanking him profusely, I left. My visit to the Shaman was the highlight of my first Canadian trip. For the rest of the time, I was busy working. Taking a four-day course is a salutary experience and a responsible one. People are attracted from varying areas of discontent. They may be divorcing, have lost children or parents or had accidents. So it is essential to be sharp as a knife, but kind too. The abuse experienced by the children who had been in Catholic orphanages was coming to court at the time. Now grown-up, some of the people who pressed charges sought solace in some cases. So did the carers of these abused children who selflessly served above and beyond the remit of their job descriptions. There were also those on the staff who found the numbers overwhelming and the stories harrowing. These were people's lives and not to be taken lightly. We have to find structures that would work for them. It might be new information, meditation practices, counselling or a change in attitude that is required. Each person is unique and convinced they are right and know all that is necessary. They don't – nor do any of us – but telling them so can be very challenging!

Returning home to Haywards Heath, I was relieved to find that everything appeared relatively normal. However, there was a letter waiting for me on the table. It was from my mother! She was not dead at all! Her sister had seen the advertisement in the newspaper and passed the information on. Apparently, she was the only other person within her childhood family who knew of my birth. The letter gave my mother's phone number and, very nervously, I called her. We talked for over an hour. She told me the whole sad story...

Her full name was Alice Hayles. She came from a strict family with a dominant father of whom she was terrified. During the war, my father James (Jim) Zimmerman was a Canadian soldier who was sent to the Isle of Wight to train on the cliffs for the Dieppe raid. He was there for less than a week. He was very tall and handsome and, when he met my mother, the inevitable occurred and I was the consequence. Then my father was very badly hurt in the Dieppe raid. He was in a body bag on the boat returning to England when someone saw it moving. He was deeply unconscious and had horrendous injuries, but he was alive! He was sent to a hospital in Birmingham and stayed there for two years. Half of his face was rebuilt and his other injuries were treated. Now pregnant, my mother went to see his Commanding Officer to explain her predicament. The man had given her a lump sum from my father's back-pay and said that was all he could do.

My mother worked as an aircraft fitter in Surrey during the war. Away from the prying eyes of her family (except for her sister who also worked on a nearby farm) she was able to have me, place me into an orphanage and return to the Isle of Wight as if nothing had happened. She was very young at the time and she told me it was all she could think to do. Later, she married a man called David Williams and had three more children, Mary, Mervyn and Helen. Her husband knew the secret from the outset, but her children never did – at least, not until they were all grown-up. She asked me to visit her, an invitation that I accepted. But I gave myself a few weeks to get used to the idea. Orphan Judy was an orphan no more, apparently!

As it worked out, I had no time to get my head round this amazing news. There was too much to keep me busy at home. Ed and Kate were going through a stormy patch. Jackie was at university, but was a regular visitor. Michael had adjusted well to his new situation, but Bronwyn was an absolute nightmare! Bunking school, over-interested in boys, staying out without any of us knowing where she was – all the usual things. She would have nothing to do with her new family and lied to us all the time about her activities. The headmaster was a regular visitor to our house, as was her social worker, but all to no avail. We all felt sorry for her, but at the same time I was also irritated on behalf of my children who had already been through so much upset themselves. Tony, now a psychologist, tried to give some guidance, but it had no impact. He also reminded me that I was in control of what happened on all fronts, so not to get overwhelmed.

Drew was now thirteen and came with me on the visit to the Isle of Wight. He was always such a lovely person, I was pleased to have him along. In fact, he was more enthusiastic about this family reunion than I was. My mother met us from the ferry. She got a shock when she saw Drew because, apparently, he looked very much like my father! We walked to her house about half an hour away, speaking only of the history of the town and other superficial things. On arrival, we met her husband, a sweet and gentle soul. He was so sympathetic toward me, holding onto my hand and looking into my eyes as he said how difficult this must be for me. Almost tearful, he wandered off into his beloved garden, taking Drew with him. To begin with, I felt awkward and somewhat resentful. I just couldn't understand how a mother could give up a child, regardless of the circumstances. I certainly could not have done that with any of mine. My mother did her best to explain and clearly she had her own issues. Perhaps not the best communicator in the world, she tried to make up for it by cooking a large lunch and showing every kindness she was able. She did give me my father's full name, rank and army number which was all the information she had about him. She talked a lot of her other children and how surprised they had been to hear about me. Then she told me she wanted to arrange a big party so that everyone could get to know each other. I said an emphatic "no". I wanted to take this slowly and not overwhelm myself or my children. Gently-gently was the name of the game.

Shortly afterwards, I went back to Canada for another two weeks' work in Montreal. This time, I took Drew with me as the people I was working for had children and there was an Arts Festival they would all be going to. I had already forwarded the details regarding my father to them. They seemed more keen on finding out what had happened to him than I did. They sent the info to the Ex-Servicemen's Association who pinned the details on their notice board. Would you believe it! My father saw the notice himself! It was the one-and-only war veterans' reunion that my father had ever attended since the war. He was tickled pink and telephoned me immediately, starting the conversation by saying no, he was not dead! He asked me to visit him, so I extended our trip by another week and agreed to fly across country to where he lived near Calgary. I was so busy, I found it easy to concentrate on work and the children's activities until we were on the five hour cross-country flight from Montreal. I had no trouble in recognising him. We looked so alike! He said we would go for coffee and drove us to the Olympic stadium where Eddie the Eagle had gained his fame. Drew loved it and was very patient as my father explained that he did know about me because his old Commanding Officer had not told him anything. Directly after he was fit for repatriation, he was flown back along with a nurse called Olive whom he had married soon after arrival. They had two children, Rodney (Rod) and Luana, one only two years younger than me. His wife had died a few years ago. Now over it, he had several girlfriends, two of whom we would meet. Quite a character, it would seem!

My father lived in a skiing town called Kimberley. He had a condominium, one of two owned by Luana and her husband, Ken. My dad had left his native Winnipeg when he'd retired from engineering and gone west. He had an interest in some land where gold was mined which he said we could visit. Drew was thrilled. We drove through Banff National Park and on for about three hours. He said he had a treat waiting for us for supper – some elk steaks he had been saving. We felt bad having to tell him we were both vegetarians, but he took it well, giving Drew some ice-cream and cheese biscuits for me, saying we would go out to breakfast the following day in town. Exhausted after our long day out, Drew fell asleep. My father and I talked on and he gave me two quick lessons in local culture. Should we meet a bear rummaging through the garbage bins, we should stand still immediately, drop the garbage and back away very slowly. We should walk backwards and not turn and run. Okay! Got that! The second lesson was if I drove anywhere, I must make sure there was a shovel, provisions, warm clothes and a sleeping bag in the boot of the car in case of a snowstorm. And, if we did get stranded, not to leave the car or try to walk for help. Got that, too! "More tomorrow," he promised, leaving me also to fall into a deep sleep.

After breakfast the following day in Kimberley, we wandered around their folk festival and stopped to listen to various singers and bands. Then, taking the ski-lift near my father's house, we went to the top of a mountain called East Kootenays and walked for hours, coming across a First Aid Hut that had been trashed by a brown bear. Seeing just what this creature could do made me heed the warning I had received the night before.

Next day we visited the gold-mining area. After making our way up a winding lane on the side of a mountain, with wood lorries hurtling down with no room to pass and the lorries unable to brake, my nerves were shot to pieces by the time we arrived. Parking and walking towards a mine, we met the dirtiest man I had ever seen in my life wearing a huge piece of rough gold around his neck on a leather thong. My father said it was worth around five thousand pounds, but the old fellow would never part with it. The weather was lovely and my father taught Drew and I to pan for gold. After two hours during which we found a couple of bits of gold dust, we started back. At least this time we were going in the same direction as the wood lorries and we returned without incident.

The following day, my half-sister Luana arrived, saying she was concerned about whether I would be able to handle all these emotional reunions. Having met me and seeing I was fine with it all, she said her concerns were allayed. We had a great time meeting dad's new girlfriends, swimming in the pool and walking the ski-trails. It was all over far too soon. Arranging to meet up again at Luana's home in a few months time, Drew and I headed back to the UK. Phew! In under six weeks, I had met both my mother and my father, both of whom I thought were dead. My children no longer just had me and each other. Now we were a part of an extended family with a huge cast of players! It was as if events had transpired to give me what I'd devoted my life to giving to others. I had my very own Second Aid! The alleviation of stress through knowledge and self-awareness was no longer just a theory. It was a living practice and I was the main beneficiary. It was wonderful!

The months passed and I returned to Canada where I met Rod. We were so alike, it was like looking in a mirror! We were living proof of the overwhelming influence of genetics and heredity in shaping our lives and personalities. We looked similar, had similar tastes and even similar opinions. Rod's wife, Mary, said it was freaky having me around – it was like living with her husband in drag! The three of us went on one of the best holidays I have ever had, sailing up the west coast of British Columbia to visit Princess Louisa Inlet and Chatterbox Falls, the latter being one of the great sights of the water world. It will remain in my memory for ever.

Back home in England, Tony and I went to meet Mervyn, my half-brother on my mother's side. He was a lighthouse keeper then working in Whitby. I found him fascinating. A gentle soul, he was a talented carpenter and a keen gardener when he was not manning his lighthouse. When we met, we had little need of words as we just 'knew' each other. Prior to this, Drew and I had been up to Oxford to meet Helen, my first maternal half-sister. She and her husband Glen were very welcoming and again we 'got on' immediately. I did not meet my other half-sister Mary for some time, but when we did there was an unconditional acceptance of each other and the whole situation that was very encouraging and impressive.

Over the next few years, I kept in touch with my mother's family and we met up as and when we were all able. To this day, we continue to get on and see each other whenever we can. Eventually Helen, Merv and Mary met my children and I met theirs. As we all lived in different parts of the UK, these meetings were fairly spasmodic, but the bond had been forged. By the time my mother died, some twelve years later, we had all completely adjusted to each other and I was part of their family. They insisted on my inclusion in everything and were so generous emotionally that I felt touched and humbled.

Meanwhile, on the other side of the Atlantic, my father also passed away around the same time. I went to his funeral. Much to my embarrassment, the priest told the story of my birth to the large congregation. The Canadians, however, saw nothing wrong with it and made me as welcome as my maternal family had done. I felt hugely sad at all the years that had been wasted not knowing my father. He was such fun and loved by everyone. But there was no going back. With the death of both my parents, one era had ended and another had begun. Just glad that I'd been able to meet and get to know both my mother and father and become part of their respective families, I turned towards the future and my continuing work with Second Aid.

Chapter 10 - Big Chiefs

With all the emotional shocks and adjustments behind me, it was time to focus on work and a personal purpose. Second Aid had gone through several phases of its own evolution. First, it was a charity, but the people attracted to it were all following their own agendas and that was not what I wanted. I have often heard tell that members of staff are the ones who really take up your time and cause problems and, with a couple of exceptions, this certainly was true in my case. Clearly it was time to try to become more business-like. A wonderful lady called Christine, who was in at the start, proved hugely helpful at keeping me on track and showing me what needed to be charged for a service that I felt should be free to one and all. Having always wanted my children to grow up to make a contribution to the community rather than just take from it, I felt I needed to lead by example. But it was impossible to be totally altruistic. Rent, living expenses and money for travel all had to be found. During my training at White Lodge, I had worked for free in many welfare establishments like prisons, abuse clinics and the like. Now, as an experienced counsellor and spiritual advisor, it was the time to offer a service to those who could mostly afford to pay for it. I felt no qualms about this. Nor did anyone else see anything wrong with it. Commercial organisations began to seek out my services along with health and welfare groups. Suddenly, I was no longer that eccentric woman with new ideas. I was being sought after as an authority on communications, awareness and group dynamics.

New opportunities were being presented to me through invitations to work in many different countries around the world. This enabled me to broaden my outlook as cultural boundaries were crossed. It was an amazing experience and one I will be forever grateful to have had. This was mirrored through work within the UK as I received more and more invitations to work for the Health Service. Medical people everywhere were coming to understand that health was more than just physical well-being. At this time, Second Aid became a limited company. Before long, many people wanted to do what I was doing and asked me to support them in working in the same way themselves. Oh, boy! Did that become a learning curve for one and all! Naively, I believed everyone would be able to do what I did with a bit of guidance – how wrong was I? Now I was dealing with clients and loving every minute of it, but I was spending enormous amounts of time and doubling my workload by going back over the work others had done because they were just not getting the results I had. Giving emotional damage limitation to clients was one thing; managing all these other issues was quite another!

After a long time, I decided to downsize by disbanding the company and just working as a self-employed consultant. What a relief that was! It felt as if the weight of history had been lifted from my shoulders. To my surprise, I seemed to be more in demand rather than less. Some deep reappraisal was called for here. What was it I wanted? I had been on a mission to pay back the kindness and care I had been shown when I had felt incapable and overextended. All through my life, someone had always shown up to help me, even if I did not realise it at the time. Peter and the staff of White Lodge were the most recent examples. I was fascinated with what caused illness and what constituted healing in all its various forms, especially why a certain type of healing appeals to one person rather than another. What I wanted to do was to give people a structure that would act like a photographic negative, enabling them to print a picture of their lives that was clear, honest and truthful to everyone concerned. This is empowering. You could liken this to using medical services such as x-rays, plastering, crutches and physiotherapy when breaking a limb. However, once the limb is healed, you should no longer need the good offices of those who have helped you. They, in turn, should let you go. What I had found was that, all too often, there were people in positions of responsibility who just wanted glory. This disempowered those they were trying to help and I considered that distasteful in the extreme.

One of my teachers at White Lodge once told me that a therapy was only as good as the rate of evolution of the person practising it. How true I found that maxim to be. I'd become somewhat critical, disillusioned and disappointed at the desire some people had to take over and dictate terms to their clients rather than working in tandem with them and supporting those who wanted to heal themselves. This was also true of those who wanted to 'fix it' for others rather than making them aware of their problems and waiting for them to fix it for themselves. After going down this path myself, I knew this was not the way to go. Time for a reappraisal and to find a new view. Living out of a suitcase and constantly travelling was beginning to lose its appeal. It was time to be more selective and to try another format.

Learning lessons in my working life was matched by doing the same in my personal life. One of the most difficult phases of parenthood is when your children try to free themselves from you and become more of who they are. Tony once said to me: "Mum, why don't you trust your upbringing of me and get off my case?" I felt suitably chastened and became much more cautious about making unasked-for comments. What I'd not expected was that, after so many years concentrating on the family and taking one step at a time to keep us all clothed, fed and together, how hard it would be to see us as free and independent units who associated by choice or not. Tony and Roberta were both very opinionated about parenthood and sure they had all the answers about bringing up children. They came to some conclusions about Tony's own upbringing and that of his siblings that were to have far-reaching consequences for our family. Oh, the arrogance of youth! Both were very keen to criticise and dispense justice. They were typically arrogant and I was the baddy! At Tony's graduation, which should have been a celebration, the atmosphere was so bad that Drew and I did not sleep a wink and left as early as we were able the following morning.

I cannot even begin to describe how painful this seeming injustice has been. Without the help of skilled therapists and meditation practice on my part, I would have sunk without trace. Having not been part of a growing-up family when I was young, my own children's experiences had been the most important and precious things to me and I loved to see them increasing. However, as they reached adulthood, all of my children were hugely different from one another and there was a parting of the ways in all but blood for many years. The wounds have now healed, but adhesions remain. Loyalty is there, as is the love, but the respect has lessened.

Thrilled by the independence and achievements of all four of my children, they became a law unto themselves, following their own paths and undertaking their own journeys. In the opinion of the other three, Drew was spoiled. However, he was the only one to be uncritical of me. He has always been unconditionally supportive and loyal to me and remains so to this day. Yes, of course, we had some falling-outs during his teenage years, but they were minor incidents. They would have remained trivial had it not been for Tony, Jackie and Heather who, through lack of experience, all thought they knew better. They are now finding out, having had children themselves, that maybe they didn't! I distanced myself until I was asked why I was doing this. Only then did I say I was no longer prepared to be treated like a leper or to be ill-treated. I would rather stay with friends who treated me well and with some respect. It took a long time for it to be comfortable to be around them once again.

Returning to my father for a moment – he had been pushing me for years to get me over to live in Canada. It proved an impossible project because, right up to the year before I appeared, the children of servicemen overseas had an automatic right of entry to Canada, got a Canadian passport and all other entitlements. All this had now been withdrawn. My father was incensed by this injustice as he saw it, saying the only way to get around the politics was to sit around in a rowing boat offshore for months on end. I didn't fancy that idea much and pointed out it might be better to stay in the UK as all the children lived there. All of a sudden it seemed like quite a good idea!

It was time to concentrate on work again and, in this, I was truly blessed. I was invited to work in Holland and Switzerland. Later, I worked in the USA and right across Canada. One day, in Toronto, I wondered if the local indigenous leaders and medicine men thought it presumptuous of me to offer spiritual services in the way I was doing. So I asked in prayer. Within days, I was invited to visit a medicine man a couple of hours away from the city. He talked with us all and then took me into his house where he plied me with teas full of herbs. Then he played a drum in my ear and I could feel the resultant vibrations throughout my body. A few months later, working in Newfoundland, I was invited to visit the local chief. A hugely busy schedule made me regretfully say no as I only had a few hours' leisure-time on one day out of the whole trip. Within an hour, his administrator was on the phone saying he would send a plane for me! I got the message – I was to visit! On the appointed day, a small plane with just the pilot showed up at St John's and off we went. After nearly an hour in the air, the pilot said to me: "There he is!" I could see this diminutive man in a white T-shirt and blue jeans waiting for us below. The pilot landed and the Chief climbed on board, greeted me and told me he was taking me to their sacred mountain. On the one hand, I was thrilled. On the other hand, I realised I was not properly dressed – white trousers were not quite the thing! The Chief did not seem to mind. We landed on a small mountain that was not our destination, the pilot not being willing to go any further with the mist being as thick as it was.

The Chief got some trail mix out of his pocket and gave me some. Then he ate some himself and held his hand out to a bird that flew onto it and started nibbling at the food. "Good gracious," I thought to myself. "I'm out with St Francis!"

Then the Chief said: "I have been taught to part the clouds, but I'm only supposed to do it in an emergency." "I don't think this classes as an emergency," I said. "I think I will be the judge of that," he replied.

Off he wandered on his own, coming back a few minutes later to tell the pilot we would fly in twenty minutes. And, sure enough, the mist lifted and we did! The plane was fitted with water-floats, so we landed on a lake and I was handed some thigh-length waders. We started to wade ashore, the Chief carrying a large rucksack. The three of us started to climb the side of another mountain. For the next hour, we walked in silence until the Chief started pointing out various points he said were 'gates' which we must observe, honour and respect. It taught me to be observant and retain my intuition at all times. Some of the gates were just two stones.

Eventually, we arrived at the top. I was told we were to perform a sacred ceremony, but first it was the peace pipe. Not having smoked for over fifteen years, I felt somewhat daunted by this. To make matters worse, when the tobacco and herbs are mixed, they are considered sacred and the entire pipe must be smoked! There were only three of us, by the time it was finished I was turning green! So I was very glad of the quiet time during prayers and just about avoided being sick. Then the Chief told the pilot to leave us as he wanted to speak with me alone. I felt flattered and humbled by the fact he was treating me as a friend. He told me my prayers had been heard and he'd been told to tell me that everyone was very happy that I was at work in their territory. They were grateful for my input and it was not considered an arrogant gesture in the least. I felt great relief on hearing this because it was something that had concerned me greatly. He shared some of his general anxieties with me and I did the same with him. It was a true soul-to-soul communication and deeply profound.

Afterwards, the pilot returned and said we must think about leaving. We left the sacred area and made our way back down the mountain in silence. On arrival at the lakeside, the Chief asked me if I would like a cup of tea. "How bizarre!" I thought, but I said, "Yes, please." So he set about chopping some dead wood from a nearby tree and made a fire. Then he whipped a teapot out of his rucksack along with some flour mixture. Soon afterwards, we had the most delicious cup of raspberry tea accompanied by home-baked bread and jam. The best meal I ever tasted in my life! Then we waded back out to the plane. We flew back to the Chief's residence and dropped him off. As I was leaving, he presented me with some handmade moccasins and some ceremonial Native American tools. "Thank you for coming," he said. "I will see you again before you leave." As I mumbled my thanks, he kissed me and waved me goodbye. Then the pilot flew me back to St John's.

For the next few days, I was fully occupied with work. So imagine my surprise when, shortly before I was due to depart, the Chief called me and said he was in the city and wanted to keep his promise to meet up again. My hectic schedules meant the only time we could meet was for breakfast the following day. What a contrast! I met him in a luxury hotel, wearing a suit! He was the First Nation Representative to the United Nations and was off to New York for a meeting. We had a wonderful couple of hours and some deep conversations, agreeing that on my next trip we should give a public talk together. This duly took place. I returned to Canada a few months later. It was in the middle of winter and the talk was scheduled to take place during the worst spell of weather you could possibly imagine. Deep snow, Arctic winds and ice everywhere! I was convinced the Chief would not make it to the venue and, even if he did, no one would show up anyway. But when the 'Management Upstairs' want something to happen, it happens! The hall was packed with well over a hundred people. Just as the organisers told me to start my talk, the Chief arrived! Neither of us had any idea what the other was going to talk about. So we just started batting the conversation between us, covering various topics of culture, ethics and healing. We found ourselves in total agreement regarding the metaphysical aspects of our work. Even though our presentations were different, there was an accord that provoked a standing ovation.

In subsequent meetings, we realised we had been gifted with a responsibility to our families and our communities to see our groups through to a level of freedom, equality and knowledge of spiritual values. This was something that was bigger than all of us. Our ways parted, but we kept in touch through a telepathic connection that we established beyond a shadow of a doubt. It is a rare privilege to meet such a person as the Chief and it has been my good fortune to meet several like him in my lifetime. Knowing them all enriched my understanding and improved the service I was able to offer to others. I continued with my workshops, usually running them myself and rarely involving others. Between times, I was busy working with individuals, either face-to-face or via the telephone or email.

One day, a friend of mine called Darryl rang me. "Are you busy?" he asked. "Not especially," I replied. "Then can you catch a plane to Luxor and meet me tomorrow?" he said. He was the organiser of a sacred tour of Egypt and the psychotherapist accompanying him had become ill and been taken to hospital. So Darryl was on his own with 20 people. This was too good an opportunity to miss, for sure. So I arrived that night, very tired, and went straight to bed in a hotel that had been booked for me. Next morning, I was woken by the call to worship from the mosques. On opening the curtains, the Nile stretched before me in both directions as far as the eye could see. I will never forget the sight! The week passed busily and quickly and proved a great success. Sadly, the person I replaced passed away. So Darryl asked me if I would consider other trips to which I said "yes".

We made a good team. I did the tour schedules and wrote them all up for the clients, the individual consultations and the group debriefings. He did all the administration, finances and organisation. For several years, these trips continued for between one and four times a year. This was in addition to all my psychotherapy work and his yoga teaching. We were fortunate enough to go to Upper and Lower Egypt several times. We also went to Greece, including many of the Greek Islands, Mexico and the USA – to name just a few. We never travelled with less than sixteen people. Sometimes, there were as many as 30. There were frequent crises including a dislocated kneecap, people losing or throwing away their visas, getting lost and many other mishaps. Yet these trips were undoubtedly worth it. To bring forward the shy and emotionally paralysed, to subdue the arrogant, to dissipate anger and to deal with people who try to control others and manipulate them to their own advantage – these were great benefits. Often, the conflicts within these groups reminded me of sibling rivalry displayed by children when they're growing up. Spiritual evolution is every bit as challenging as emotional and physical growth, without a doubt!

Embracing everyone but, at the same time, not putting up with any nonsense from anyone is a hard balance to strike. It's way too easy to be walked all over if you are not careful. That is something I have had to learn. If you are too nice, people will like you, but you do not put yourself in a position to tell the truth and help them. On the other hand, being too blunt and making people dislike you can destroy the trust needed for any meaningful relationship to work properly. You have to pitch somewhere between the two. Years of non-stop work had proved this to my satisfaction. If clients did not agree with what I told them, then they would have to find out for themselves in the fullness of time there was nothing more I could do. Trying to 'rescue' others is a fool's errand. Certainly, we can put ourselves in their pathway and act as a way marker, but if they take no notice of us then, at a certain point, we have to let go.

Around this time, I moved to Majorca. Heather lived there already and had not been having an easy time of it. Drew, being between jobs, had gone to support her. While he was there, he did odd jobs for friends, one of which was in a beautiful property with a large garden. When I visited to see how both of them were getting on, he said he must show this place to me. He felt it would make an ideal Retreat Centre that could support my work and enable me not to travel as much as I had been doing. I had a friend with me called Bridget and we visited at dusk one wet, cold evening and were very impressed. We went back the next morning to take another look prior to our leaving.

As we travelled home, we talked about this building and its location a great deal. Bridget suggested we should enlist the advice of others and I recalled someone who had pushed and pushed and said if I ever found anywhere they would fund it. I knew there would be agendas attached to this, but at Bridget's insistence I called anyway. My approach was enthusiastically received, to say the least. The person involved, who was called Lorna, said she would need to clear it with members of a family Financial Trust. They subsequently visited and a purchase was made with alacrity on the proviso I would head up the new centre for a minimum of two years. To me, heading it up meant guiding policy and working myself. This I did. While I was running successful and well-attended courses, Heather was duly employed by the Trust to do the housekeeping and general care along with handling bookings. We worked really hard, interfacing and covering for each other. There were only the two of us doing everything required.

Having been lucky enough to elicit a lot of goodwill by our hard work, others stepped in to help us. They were sorely needed on one occasion when Heather really hurt her back by falling down the stairs outside the Centre. Even so, she still managed to cook meals at home and a couple of guys collected them, served them and cleared up. For me, it was impossible to be in the lecture hall running the course and do anything else at the same time. Fortunately, we managed to interest and involve some local people by organising a meditation group and this led to further inquiries about using the facility. The Trust member responsible for the finance so wanted inclusion and involvement that her demands for attention were handled mainly by my daughter for the only things to discuss were the more practical issues.

When the two years had passed, I was aware that my clients needed me to visit them as well as their coming to the Centre in Majorca. It was amazing that people had travelled from as far as Australia, Canada, Scandinavia and the UK for as long as they had. But unless I visited other places and enlarged the market, I knew I could not sustain the viability of the business. Courses run by colleagues were not so successful and the income of the Centre was resting heavy on my shoulders.

However, I stayed for another two years before saying I'd had enough. By that time, holiday lettings were sustaining us through the hot summer months. Heather handled these with the Trust that was obviously keen to make money and maintain upkeep.

As the Trust became more and more involved with the property, it seemed I was being squeezed out. Few of the Trust members fully understood the spiritual work I was doing and it quickly sank to a low priority. A beginning always carries an ending within it and vice versa. One of the Trust members got married in the garden of the premises and subsequently decided to move there with her new husband and live in the house. The only option for them was to rent out the other half of the house to holiday-makers to generate income. This made the accommodation way too small to house groups on courses. So the decision was made. Heather would continue to be employed by the Trust but I, as they say, was superfluous to requirements. Time to move on again – and something of a relief!

Chapter 11 - Conclusions

Watching your beloved children as they begin to shoulder their own responsibilities and face hard lessons of living is as bad, if not worse, than doing it yourself. The name of this new game is detachment which is not the same at all as not caring. It does involve new learning, not least how to let go and enjoy yourself. This gives you and others the freedom they need to find a way that works for them in their own time and in their own way. Loving support when asked for, a truthful response if requested, otherwise keep quiet and get on with what you are doing yourself. And give all others the freedom to do the same!

Phew! What a journey to date! Time to sit down and conduct a live post-mortem, perhaps. I would consider the family journey to be the inner core of what I do and who I am, whereas the work-related journey is the exterior mirror. Finally, the two are being integrated together. Since returning to the UK, it is so easy to see the beauty of nature – even in the middle of a cold winter.

It is easy to be grateful for kindness and courtesy shown. Resentment that another person might have a better or a different remit never occurs to me, only gratitude that we have been delivered safely to where we all are now. Tony is working as a lecturer at one of the major universities in the UK. He has a family of his own and has run all of the big five marathons in a single year. Jackie is a producer and commissioning editor for TV, married with two beautiful boys. Heather runs a property management service and has a charming mischievous daughter. And Drew is a paramedic married to the loveliest wife ever. How sweet is that? The bitter pills that had to be swallowed on occasions to achieve this have turned out to be sugar-coated for sure, even though I might not have thought so at the time!

I should also mention here that Betty had finally died. It happened as Drew and I were returning from a standard visit to her and were called back to the hospital. She died on the operating table having a hip fixed after a fall. All the children and their partners went to a simple funeral service in Sidmouth Parish Church, then on to the Crematorium in Exeter. Afterwards, we had a coffee and a sandwich in a nearby hotel and all went back to our respective homes or work. I felt we honoured her as best we were able, but none of us seemed unduly affected – including me. She was a person who was unable to meet the need of others. This was not really her fault, just how she was. Years before, I had already detached myself from any emotional ties with her, but I could not disassociate myself completely. I felt Jane and I owed her a debt of gratitude of sorts. Jane did not come over from Australia for the ceremony. She just told me to buy some flowers. I agreed that was enough.

It is easy to see the glass is half empty when you're feeling somewhat worn down and fatigued. Our body will sometimes remind us in a manner that can feel quite brutal that we need to rest and recover, reflect, update and upgrade information and catch up with where we are now. It's not resentment, just fatigue, which requires the body to rest and recover.

Externally I learned though travelling and varying challenges which forced me to pray, to meditate, to ask questions and to keep seeking answers. Eventually I looked within. Tired of feeling a casualty, getted patched up for a repeat performance I wanted to anchor to the Earth all I had learned. Time to let go and free myself from soul pain and if successful to offer that learning onto others in the form of Second Aid.

Why was that necessary? I had been programmed to be good and to comply with others' wishes and to disregard myself since birth. I tried to do so but, as a result, unwittingly cut myself out of the equation. It was almost as if I had set myself apart from the main story. Not wanting to get in the way of others' progress is one thing; total disregard of yourself is quite another. I was not unhappy, but I had been sickened by the sadness and disappointment that had been experienced. Certainly, I had been frightened on occasions and may well have taken on the fear of those I loved as well. I never wanted anyone around me to feel not wanted, not cared for, not respected, not loved or not included. I had been angry at circumstances and sometimes with people who appeared to think 'they knew it all' and who tried to bully me or my children as a result. Why should one have to commend loyalty? Isn't it really and truly a natural state? No wonder people get cynical when there appears to be so little time and so little trust or loyalty when occasion demands.

I also realised that I had made some sound choices as well as foolish ones in my earlier life. Other people may want to embrace negatives. I didn't and still don't. I understand they are there on occasion, but only as an invitation to convert them into positives and not something to get bogged down by. Why isn't this sort of thing taught in school? Communication within ourselves is hard enough before we start communications with others. We don't always need to recycle the same old junk. It can be put to use. But to use it just needs the courage and commitment to re-embrace it, to extract what we need from it, then to release the residual. Without really understanding what I had done, I realised I had changed my beliefs and that it is impossible to do so without having the right attitude. I had adapted to physical limitations and understood the implications nearly always in hindsight rather than foresight – but that is good enough.

Now it was time to change and be changed once more. This requires a reality check so that, instead of being dragged along kicking and screaming, the choices are more willingly made. When Tony was eighteen, I made him a cake in the shape of a book. On one side I wrote 'Chapter 1 is done' on the other side 'Chapter 2 is new'. He was off to join the Navy and life would change. I felt like this now for myself. There was no way I could go on teaching or counselling. I was saturated, burned out and did not trust myself not to be facetious. Alternatively, it was tempting to go into a rant along the lines of: "If you think you've got problems, then let me tell you some of the ones I've had! Why don't you just stop moaning and get on with living?" Not wanting to mistreat the vulnerable like that, I thought maybe I'd better quit while ahead and find another way of working.

Wanting to fulfill my responsibilities but not wanting to push anybody around, wanting to pull my weight but not wanting to be found wanting, I approached a friend and mentor who said: "The answer is easy. Write a book outlining all of your Second Aid techniques and then leave people to do it for themselves if they want to."

"Good idea," I thought. Quite easy, too. All the material was written down already as a result of keeping detailed course notes. It was just a matter of putting it together and in an order that made sense. Approaching a publisher, it was encouraging to be told what to do. "Get an editor," he said. "You need a fresh pair of eyes and to work on it until both of you like the result." Then he added: "By the way, everyone and their mother goes on a weekend course and sets themselves up as wise and all knowing. It would really work if you wrote down your own story, adding family information, then no one could doubt you knew what you were talking about."

Saying I didn't want to do this because I was a very private individual did me no good at all. "If you really want to support, encourage and assist others and you don't want to teach, you'll have to, wont you?" he explained. My next objection didn't work, either! "I don't want to invade the children's privacy," I argued. "They've had enough of that through my work, anyway. Everyone thought it to be their right to comment or question them when they could not locate me. My work was my choice and not theirs and they should be allowed to make their own choices without my interference. That much is clear." "So change their names in the book so no one could trace them and do it anyway," he advised.

A "Shall I/Shan't I" dialogue ensued. Eventually, it was my brother Mervyn who helped me to decide. He had done me the favour of buying me a car ferry ticket as it was easy for him to do and that was how I came to understand that my driving licence had expired. I said to him: "Oh, your sister is an idiot!" Later in the conversation he asked what I had meant, ready to jump to defend his two full sisters and not realising I had been referring to myself. Yes, there was a twinge of pain at this, but also a huge regard and respect for the welcome and inclusion they all had gifted me with, both the Canadians and Celts alike. Suddenly, I felt I owed it to everybody to tell my story.

Many are wounded by war, but if we want to live in peace we have to work at it. Wounds will only heal if we let them. Doing this work would open me to the armchair observations of others who would misunderstand, reinterpret and modify according to their codes of understanding, then tell me I was misguided or even wrong. Being a teacher means we need to learn as well, but could I be bothered to go around the circuit yet again?

Life has a funny way of pushing us to do things. A good friend of mine called Les who is a doctor of medicine was talking to me one day and said: "I wish you would write a book on the things that prompt people to get the various diseases we have been discussing." Days later, having lunch with Darryl, he said: "A coffee table book on all the Sacred Tours we have done would make good reading and be beautiful." Yes, OK! I get the message! I decided to just get on and write the one I'm just finishing right now! I had died to the old way of doing things in the last chapter and was being born to the new one right here and right now within life. Get over it and get on!

Whether I look on it as a 'stitch up' or not, it is a happening event. One part of my own insecurity in the past was the feeling of being inadequate to meet demand. Another was my pronounced intuitive ability where I so often 'knew' ahead of time how someone would behave or respond. Although I had half-heartedly written some of the text for a book about my life, it seemed I was to be moved back to the UK to finish it. In meditation, I got the name of the town. Within days of this, two people knocked on my door in Majorca when I was hard at work in the office. It was a real estate agent saying two Danes wanted to buy my house and were asking, "Is it for sale?" Events moved at breakneck speed after that. The agent brought these two lovely Danish people to view along with their children and it was clear they were going to make an offer. In due course, they did and it was a good one. The sale was facilitated by a skilled and loving Spanish lawyer called Jacobo whose family I had known for the eight years I'd lived in Majorca. Because we all wanted an honorable and ethical sale, we agreed that we should all use the services of the same lawyer, allowable under Spanish law. It all went like clockwork without a harsh word anywhere. There could not have been any more courtesy and honourable care anywhere. It still amazes me that, in a depressed market with no one buying or selling anything very much, this all happened without any effort on my part in the space of eight short weeks. I had to leave the Balearics one week prior to the completion date as there was to be a delay of a week as a result of the Danes' bank transfer. No problem – Jacobo had power of attorney and acted on my behalf, both he and the buyers advising me all was well and done within minutes of each other. Where was I? At Mervyn's 60th birthday party, just as I'd promised I would be some two years earlier!

I phoned one of my good friends, Pav, to let off some steam about my sudden move back to Britain. She laughed with me and assured me the town stated within the UK was not so bad and actually had some points of appeal. She looked it up online and was telling me some of the attractions. I was underwhelmed! It took some getting used to and I needed to protest and have my little tantrum before agreeing to visit the area. Initially, I stayed with some friends, Julie and Martin, but I also took the opportunity to visit Jackie and Drew together with their families. What a pleasure this was and I was very touched at how pleased they seemed to be to see me.

So off I went to Wiltshire. No expectations, but I did visit the various estate agents and buy the local paper. Some of them were unpleasant or indifferent. Others were helpful, but didn't seem to have a clue as to what might be suitable, probably because I didn't know myself. But there was one property (and you only need one) that I liked on walking through the door. It was as appropriate as the agents had said it would be.

"This is too easy!" I thought. Better suffer and be thorough and look at least another 20 houses or so. Seven days later, I was back again to have another look at the original house, this time with Julie who was experienced in business. We both agreed it was ideal and had all of the things I needed. Suggesting I make what to me seemed a very low offer and bound to be refused, I did so and on the contrary it was accepted! Oh, my goodness! What next? Some building work. One thing I was absolutely sure of, I did not want anyone including myself to be exploited. Yet, as usual, the cowboys were there and I had to get beyond them to those who were genuine in their skill area. Was what we were doing 'fit for purpose' within any and every area? Certainly challenges were occurring! The family visited and liked what they saw. Close friends expressed their interest and desire to involve themselves. It was a done deal again so quickly.

Then Martin found an ideal car for me to drive and I so enjoy the beautiful countryside and the space. It brings out every reason to love the earth within its wholeness and its holiness. Time to anchor and focus on the work in hand. As more and more people have extreme experiences, maybe all this material should be made into an easier form of reference. Maybe I would write both books and so unite the two facets and enable others to have the courage to follow their star and live their dream. It would be a less hands-on experience, yet it could be an encouragement to others facing challenges. "You have got to be kidding!" had been my initial, ungracious response, but I was coming around to the idea! But now here we are and I've got to say I have realised that I am both adequate and worthy. All is well and many wonderful people have moved in to support this endeavor as others did in the past, one way or another. Some are there to goad me, some to encourage, some to ridicule, some for their own purposes and others to promote mine. What a tapestry! Let's hope it makes a beautiful picture which supports all and harms no one.

Also by Judy Fraser

Second Aid

In the mid-Eighties, following an intensive seven-year course at the College Of Spiritual Psychotherapeutics near Tunbridge Wells in Kent and a further seven years giving talks and running courses under its auspices, Judy struck out on her own. She formed *Second Aid*, an organisation dedicated to providing support to people in times of emotional crisis through the media of counselling, meditation, prayer, discussion and increased self-awareness. People suffering from a whole host of problems like bereavement, grief, stress, abuse and relationship failures were given help and guidance to deal with their difficulties, resolve them and find inner peace. It's a service for which many thousands of people will be eternally grateful for her intuition and wisdom. And now this wealth of experience is going to be available in the form of a self-help manual. Judy kept detailed notes of her work over the years. These are now being used to prepare a volume of help and advice for people who still need the benefit of her wisdom but cannot seek it personally.

www.judyfraser.com